WHAT'S YOUR POINT?

WHAT'S YOUR POINT?

A Proven Method For Giving Crystal Clear Presentations!

By Bob Boylan

Edited by Norine Larson
Illustrated by Jack Lindstrom

Point
Publications

1st Edition

Copyright © 1988, 1989 by Bob Boylan

Point Publications
3701 Shoreline Drive - Suite 106
Wayzata, Minnesota 55391

Printed in The United States of America

Library of Congress Cataloging in Publication Data
        Boylan, Bob, 1936 —
        What's Your Point?

        Bibliography: p.
        Includes index
        1. Public Speaking. I. Larson, Norine, 1941
            II. Title.
        PN4121.B5935 1987 808.5'1   87-6952
        ISBN 0-941755-01-0

This book is dedicated to you, Mom. Throughout your 37 year career as a teacher, as well as during your retirement years, your entire being has always searched for better ways to think about things — better ways to do things.

Then you would change ... and get better.

That's what this book is all about.

ACKNOWLEDGEMENTS

The key people who have made this book a reality are the people I have trained. They have tried my ideas ... and found success. They have given me ideas to improve my facilitation ability as well as my knowledge.

Norine Larson has been extremely valuable in recapsulizing my thoughts to be concise and clear for this first book. Nancy Miller proved to be very helpful as an "over-view editor" to keep us clear and structured. Jack Lindstrom's creative mind helped to make this book visually interesting, as well as fun to read.

Our company, LaserPrint, set all the type. Susan Smart and June Gongoll did great work to maximize readability.

The self-publishing effort was led by Kathy Oberhauser, a major organizational triumph.

A special thanks to my wife Judy for encouraging me to "tell my story" regarding Presentation Skills. I love her for her trust in me.

ABOUT THE TITLE

After completing this book, the title came to me during a Presentation Workshop I was conducting at a company.

A participant had just completed a presentation and we were all viewing the video tape. After the tape was played, one of the workshop participants asked the presenter, "Bill ... I really didn't understand your ideas ... they were confusing ... *what was your point anyway?"*

It became so clear to me that this question ... *"what's your point?"* to a presenter is the *bottom line*.

Since this is a book for business people, to help them become better presenters ... I'm anxious to show you how to make crystal clear presentations ... so your listener doesn't say ... **"what's your point?"**

Bob Boylan

"The real stars are the people who

can get the organization moving. This book will help you get things done. It will help you sell your ideas ... and gain corporate commitment and action. This book is not just how to present well ... it is about how to present successfully!"
Mike McGrath — President
Time Inc. Canada Ltd.

"Full of invaluable techniques

and ear catching humor. The POV exercises are really the core of your ideas ... and have made our presentations crisp, focused and attention grabbing."
Jack Stone — Vice President International Operations
NUS Corporation — Washington, D.C.

"Bob's book reflects his style

of enthusiasm and having fun while you learn some very practical skills. His methods and ideas are directly responsible for increasing the effectiveness of presentations here!"
Richard Collier — Manager Development & Training
Northern States Power Company — Minneapolis

"The bottom line

is Bob Boylan's ideas work. His method shows you how to convey ideas clearly, concisely and with understanding."
Gary Bratlund — President
The Executive Committee – Minneapolis

"I finally discovered the Boylan Method

— It in itself is such a BGO (Blinding Glimpse of the Obvious). Now my presentations are more clear, concise and focused. This book is now a "must read" for me annually."
Ann Boden — Senior Vice President
McKim Advertising — Toronto

CONTENTS

COMMITMENT TO CONTENT

FINE TUNING

FOREWORD

This is not just a book on giving crystal clear presentations; it's a book that helps you to get people to agree with you, make a decision and do something.

In most big companies today the real stars are the people who can get the organization moving. Good ideas are great, getting them accomplished is spectacular. This book will help people get things done. It will help them sell their ideas and gain corporate commitment and action.

Ninety percent of middle and senior managers spend more than fifty percent of their time selling — to get resources, agreements, action or commitment. It's internal selling, the most important kind. The forum is management or committee meetings and the sales pitch is usually a presentation. This book is not just about how to present well; it is about how to present successfully.

Bob is one of the best teachers I've met. I've had him give workshops to both my staff and my best customers. They raved about the effect and, even more surprising, they changed as a result.

Time Magazine has used Bob Boylan's talents in Canada, the U.S. and Europe. Based on the excellent results, I bet we'll also use him in Asia.

Bob's ideas can make you more successful and make you like yourself better. The first step is to read what he has to say. Then you have to risk a little and try some new approaches. For me it was well worth the change.

Michael J. McGrath
President
Time Canada, Ltd.

INTRODUCTION

In working with companies across the country, two things have become very clear:

1. Business people focus on content in their meetings.

2. Business people want to communicate their competence in all their meetings. It is what they're paid for and most likely the reason they were invited to the meeting.

Our method has one goal — to help business people be better presenters. It takes you where you are — content oriented — and, with a three point method, brings you to where you want to be — a better presenter. It is a natural, attainable goal. There are not 59 things to remember, just 3.

You will be a better presenter if you develop these three things:

1. Focused Content
2. Correct Content
3. Commitment to the Content

This book details how you can use these three ideas in all your presentations. We know when you put them to work for you, you will enjoy the benefits of being a clear, interesting and energized presenter.

I am not the normal speech teacher or drama coach. I'm a businessman. I know business people are busy people; this book is written to accommodate you. It's easy, moves quickly and, most importantly, gives you the tools you need.

Bob Boylan

CHAPTER 1

WHY PRESENTATION SKILLS

A retired carpenter goes into the confessional and says,
"Father, I stole some lumber."
"What did you do with it, my son?"
"Well, Father, I built a bird house."
"Doesn't seem like a big deal!"
"Well, Father, I stole some more lumber."
"What did you do with it?"
"I built a dog house."
"That's not too bad."
"But, Father, I stole some more lumber."
"What did you do with it?"
"I built a garage."
"That's a lot of lumber - that's a serious sin. I want you to make a novena."
"You want me to make a novena, Father?"
"That's right, my son!"
"OK, Father, I'll tell you what. If you can come up with a plan for it, I can probably get the lumber."

Two people are in a situation where they supposedly should understand each other. But they don't. To a retired carpenter, "make a" means "build a." To the priest anyone in a confessional obviously knows about the prayer form called a novena.

That's how difficult communication is!

I wish I were as good at communicating as I'd like to be, but like you I'm just a "tryer." I make my living helping people get better. In our seminars, we joke about the mistakes we can make because of poor communication.

As you pass the registration desk in hotels, there's a sign that says

> # REST ROOMS
> # USE STAIRS

Imagine the trouble you'd get into if you did!

Or how about the sign inside the bathroom of hotel rooms?

> ## PUT SHOWER CURTAIN INSIDE TUB
> ## BEFORE TAKING SHOWER

If you really do that, give yourself some extra time. It takes about twenty minutes to take those little things off the top of the curtain.

So, even when they're printed, our communications aren't clear.

PRESENTATION DEFINED

The form of communication I've specialized in is the **Presentation**.

The <u>Presentation</u>
- by definition -
You ask
somebody to agree with
you, make a decision or to
do something.

The presentation is *not* information sharing. You don't want it to end with the audience just saying "Thank you." You expect something to happen. You are asking somebody to do something, to make a decision or change a behavior. This can be done one-on-one, seated in an office or with a team of people in front of a large group. It is what you are doing in business all the time.

Estimates are that **94% of an executive's day is spent in communications-related activities.** Fifty-three percent of these communications involve face-to-face meetings. Yet, fewer than 1% of people in business focus any attention on developing their presentation skills after they leave college. And few colleges offer more than the required speech class.

Most people worry more about teaching their dogs to speak than about helping themselves learn to speak better.

> "The ability to express an idea is well nigh as important as an idea itself."
> Bernard Baruch

Why bother to improve your presentation skills? Because as a business person you are concerned about benefits.

BENEFITS OF GOOD PRESENTATIONS

Benefit Number 1

If you are a good presenter, you are clear and concise.

You won't talk long. You'll be crisp and people will know what you're talking about. In today's fast world, it is imperative that all our presentations — whether one-to-one or one-to-fifty — be clear, concise and organized. **No one has time for repeat meetings made necessary because the message wasn't clear the first time.**

Benefit Number 2

If you are a good presenter, you are in control.

Something in a presentation will always screw up. Slides won't work, things will fall off the wall or the key decision maker will leave to take a phone call. When you're in control, the effect of these situations will be minimized. When they do happen, you'll know how to handle them.

Benefit Number 3

When you are a good presenter, you have more authority.

Whether you stand up to say something or stay seated, you have to have some presence in front of people. Presence is mostly visual. If you're a good presenter, people will see you as a leader, one with authority. If you're a leader in your company but a poor presenter, you don't have that presence. You have a problem! No one will follow and by definition the leader has to have someone following.

Benefit Number 4

When you are a good presenter, more action will be taken on your recommendations.

More action means more success and that's the bottom line, isn't it? The whole idea is to make your communication more effective so that you get more action. For some of you that means getting more orders. When people understand what you say, more things will happen.

A friend of mine, Wally Faster, sits in the executive offices of General Mills. I asked him, "Wally, how important are presentation skills?" Listen to what he said.

"We have all kinds of highly skilled and motivated people here at General Mills. If I want to spend ten million dollars to create something, we have experts in finance, marketing, operations, R & D — you name it. We have MBA's and others with all kinds of expertise, but . . .

"There is a wide difference between a person's competence and a person's effectiveness based on their ability to communicate verbally."

The human resource department of your company probably didn't make a mistake when they hired you. You are not incompetent! The difficulty is getting the competence out. I work with all kinds of people, and I can assure you that the major frustration they express is getting their competence from their brain to somebody else's. **Competence isn't the problem, communication is.** We are paid to be effective. We are paid to produce, not just to show up. If we're not effective, we should be off the payroll.

*Not long ago, a man about 55 was in
one of my Presentation Skill Workshops.
He stood up and did his assigned presentation
about his job. Seven colleagues were sitting
around the table participating in the
exercise of critiquing their video taped
presentations.
One of the people said to him, "Walt, I didn't
quite understand what you were saying there."
He replied, "Yah, I don't know how to put it."
I said, "Walt, how long have you been
with this company?"
He said, "25 years."
I said, "Walt, it's time you learn how to put it."*

It's time we all learn how to put it!

What Do You Fear Most?

From ***People's Almanac Presents the Book of Lists***

1. Speaking Before A Group

2. Heights

3. Insects & Small Bugs

4. Financial Problems

5. Deep Water

6. Sickness

7. Death

8. Flying

9. Loneliness

10. Dogs

The one reason people would rather die than speak in public is that they have not been trained. It's not too late to start — unless you prefer to die!

SKILLS NEEDED

We have found that most people have the actual skills needed for good presentations. What they need to know is how to transfer these skills. Those comfortable techniques used in small meetings need to be brought to the large group. Conversely, the organization, preparation and audio-visuals used for the large group will greatly improve the one-on-ones.

Skills you use naturally when presenting one-on-one:

Skills you use naturally when presenting to a large group:

Eye Contact
Calm, Relaxed
Vocal Energy
Story Telling
Natural

} Bring all these to both situations {

Use of
Audio-visuals
Organization
Preparation

The Boylan Method of presenting has been developed after years of helping business people present. It's a method that can be used for all your presentations to make maximum use of your time. **If you use it, you will be better.**

**It's time to learn a new skill.
Good communication is a skill.
It is learnable!**

About 8 months ago, our pastor, a sixty year-old Benedictine — wisdom personified, and full of energy — made a remark I've borrowed.

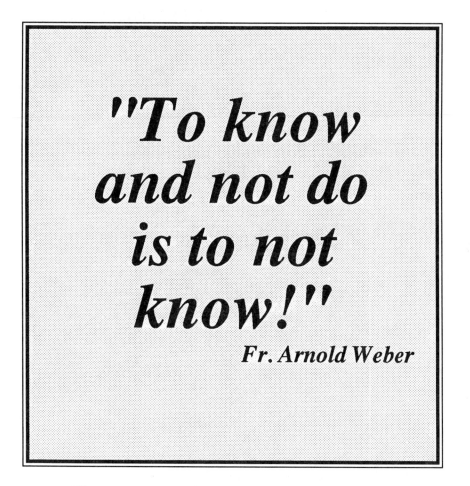

"To know and not do is to not know!"

Fr. Arnold Weber

Chances are you have all the individual techniques you need. We want to encourage you to begin now to use them in a new way — to begin to **"do"**.

This will take some risk on your part. But only when you risk will you get better.

BGOs

When we set out to learn, we need to make sure our brains are open to learning. If they are too full to take in a new idea, maybe it's time for some old ideas to leave.

One way to do it is to keep a list of BGOs as you go through this book. BGO stands for

Blinding Glimpse of the Obvious

BGOs are those things that cause you to say, "Jeez, I really never thought of it like that." Capture BGOs. Write them down. Do something with them!

This page is here for you to record your own BGOs about presenting.

Bend, staple or mutilate this page so you can find it easily and come back to it as you read. Use more paper if you need to, but record all you find.

1.
_____

2.
_____

3.
_____

4.
_____

5.
_____

6.
_____

7.
_____

8.
_____

9.
_____

10.
_____

11.
_____

12.
_____

13.
_____

14.
_____

15.
_____

A BGO is a BGO only if you act on it!

SUMMARY

- You need presentation skills for clear, concise communications.

- Good presentation skills give you more authority and control.

- More action is taken on your recommendations when you're a good presenter.

- Presentation skills are learnable.

- To learn new skills, your brain has to be open to learning.

- It takes some personal risk to get better in this skill.

- BGOs can provide an action plan.

CHAPTER 2

FOCUS - WHO AND WHERE?

Every one of us likes to come out of a meeting saying, "I got a lot out of that meeting." As a presenter, we always want to make that happen.

Abraham Lincoln had a fantastic quote. "When I get ready to talk to people, I spend two/thirds of the time thinking what they want to hear and one/third thinking about what I want to say."

There are three major variables when we make presentations.

YOU	You know you. But do you know you in relationship to the other people?
CONTENT	We tend to spend all our time here. This is the easy part.
THE AUDIENCE	Spend more time here. It's the only reason you are speaking.

The audience — whether one person or one hundred — is more willing to satisfy your needs if they see a gain in it for themselves.

AUDIENCE ANALYSIS

We don't spend enough time analyzing who we're speaking to. Identifying the audience begins with **a basic demographic profile.**

 How many people will be there?

 What is the ratio of men to women?

 What is their age range?

 What do you know about their cultural background?

 What is their level of education?

Before you work on your content, you have to have answers to these questions. For many in-house meetings, the answers are easy. The audience is so familiar you know each title, salary and idiosyncrasy. Mentally then, define them as subordinates or superiors and by the role they play in the organization.

If you do not have this information at your fingertips, GET IT. Ask questions, call the secretary, talk to the person who gave you this assignment.

Analyzing and identifying your audience can totally change the **words** of your presentation. (Have you ever sat through a presentation where so much "in-house jargon" was used that you thought you were hearing a foreign language.)

The next area of concern should be **the listener's relationship to your topic.** Audiences bring a lot of background with them, along with some definite opinions. The more of this you can get your hands on, the more you can use it to your advantage. Consider these questions:

 How much does your audience already know about this topic?

 Do I know any of their opinions on the issue?

 Does your audience have an attitude about you? What is it?

 Have they had any personal experience with your topic?

When you have these answers, the most important question you have to face as a presenter is the one every person in the audience is asking: **What's in it for me?** Each person is listening to you in terms of his or her own vested interests. **What's in it for me?** The audience members are deciding what your idea means for them.

WHAT'S IN IT FOR ME?

**Your Audience is Tuned to
Station WIIFM —
What's In It For Me.**

TYPES OF AUDIENCES

When your audience analysis is complete, you will be able to mentally categorize them according to their attitude toward you. Whether the audience is one person or fifty, they will fall into one of three categories:

Respectful

Neutral

Hostile, Resistant or Defensive

The **respectful** audience can be described as those people who either already know you or who respect you just because of the introduction. (Most CEO's fall into this category.) It becomes your responsibility not to let your title do all the work. You need to deliver! Too many "titled" people talk too long, are not organized or are just plain boring! It is your job to fulfill the respect given you by being a clear, concise and impactful communicator!

Neutral is the position most audiences take when they face presenters. The presenter's job then is to build credibility — it will not just be freely given. You have the competence to handle the situation. Good speaking skills will let this competence build the credibility you need.

AGENDA FOR HOSTILE AUDIENCE

Defensive, resistant or hostile groups are the ones with whom we least want to deal, but they can be reached with a special agenda.

1.   Admit The Differences

You're back in a meeting with your manager. At the last meeting you proposed a restructuring of his department, for what you see to be, greater efficiency. He was quite vocal in his opposition. You want to maintain your relationship with this person, but your job necessitates that you try again. Now he's back in your office. You say, "Last week when we got together, I proposed an idea for restructuring your department. You said you didn't like the idea — in fact, you were quite verbal about it. If I remember correctly, you gave these reasons —" — and you list the reasons. "Is that right?" The manager says,"You betcha — and you forgot one more."

What you've just done is given him credibility. He knows you heard him. You and he are now mentally sitting side by side looking at the problem.

Too many second meetings start with the presenter hoping to win over the audience by listing the two or three benefits that were forgotten at the last meeting. All that does is build even higher the wall between you and the audience. The listener wonders why you didn't listen at the last meeting. You've told him he doesn't matter.

Most arguments are not 90-10.
Most are 51-49.

There is probably some room in the differences for you to find agreement if you put yourself in the listener's moccasins. Verbalize any common ground you can find.

2.   Present Your Opponent's Favorable Arguments

"Mr. Manager, quite frankly, if I were in your shoes, I'd go along with points 3 and 4." By telling the person how you feel, you're telling him you don't think he's stupid. His arguments have validity. By building the bridge between you, you've laid the foundation to have him listen to you. You can now ask him to look objectively at the proposal from a new position.

3.   Appeal to Your Opponent's Objectivity

The once-hostile audience is now more willing to trust you because you've let him know you've heard him. You can now go ahead with your presentation.

No matter which type of audience you face, it is important to know that they have come with their own agenda. When you're preparing your content, you have to keep their agenda in mind.

Listener's Agenda

1. **What's the point?**

2. **What's in it for me?**

3. **Now what?**

THE SETTING

Part of the necessary preparation for your talk involves the "where". Where is your talk going to be given? What does the room look like?

Most speakers overlook the important fact that <u>the speaker, not the listeners, is responsible for the physical surroundings</u>.

This does not mean you have to set up chairs, etc., but it does mean you'd better know exactly what's in there and give directions on how you want it set up. Draw out the surroundings exactly the way you wish them to be, and then make it happen.

Ideally for small presentations, get into a room <u>without tables</u> — this includes a desk. **A desk can be a barrier between people.** Many of our clients raise the concern that the presentation needs to be in their superior's office where the physical setting is quite established. Are you sure that's the way it has to be? Have you tried to change it? What would happen if you said, *"I know we usually meet in your office, but to use your time most efficiently for my presentation, I'd like to meet in room A."*

A desk can be a barrier between two people trying to communicate.

When the meeting is small, it is also wise to determine who will sit where. The chief decision maker should be positioned with the best view of you and your materials. Don't assume you can't make this happen. A simple *"I know you usually sit there, Mr. Chairman, but today it's more beneficial for you to sit over here"* will usually work.

Many presentations fail because the physical set-up, not the content, botched it up. The flip chart wasn't there, there was no microphone, the overhead bulb was burnt out. Don't let that happen. Take charge! Make the physical surroundings yours!

Many of our clients make presentations as teams. In that situation, a time line is a necessary part of your physical preparation. It clarifies jobs and eliminates time-consuming overlaps. This is one we've used successfully.

	DATE DUE	PERSON RESPONSIBLE
Presentation Strategy		
Presentation Agenda		
Information Gathering		
Visual Aids		

THE BASICS —

A Checklist for Audience and Setting

This chart lists what we call "the basics" that fall under the responsibility of the presenter. Don't let an unattended "basic" foul up your presentation.

THE AUDIENCE

Correct Spelling of Names
Correct Titles
Key Decision Maker(s)
Background
- A. Job History
  - By Company   • By Responsibility
- B. Most Recent Success in Business
- C. Personal Interests
- D. Family Information
- E. Education

Any Idiosyncrasies of People ... i.e., Dress, "Scared Cows," Buzz Words, etc.

THE SETTING

- Size of Room
- Wall Surfaces for Pinning and Taping
- Window Coverings
- Lighting
- Power
- Access to Rehearse
- Access to Set Up/Take Down
- Sound Needs
- Sound Problems
- Room Arrangement Flexibility
- Coffee/Coke Service
- Chalk Trays to Display Materials
- The Correct Number of Chairs and Tables
- Audio Visual Needs

"THE PROS DO THE BASICS WELL EVERY DAY"
Vince Lombardi

Joel Weldon, a speaker from Scottsdale, Arizona, summarized physical preparation with this concept in a presentation to the National Speakers' Association, July 28, 1981:

Have you ever been stung by a mosquito?

Have you ever been stung by a bee?

**Have you ever been bitten by a gnat
or a "no-see-um"?**

Have you ever been bitten by an elephant?

**IT'S THE LITTLE THINGS
THAT GET YOU!**

Physical preparation of the room is one of
those "little things."

SUMMARY

- An audience analysis is a necessary step in the preparation of a presentation.

- The audience members are tuned to station WIIFM: What's In It For Me?

- You can reach a hostile audience with a special agenda.

- The speaker is responsible for the physical preparation of the room where the talk is given.

- Lack of room preparation can destroy your presentation.

- In even the smallest presentation it is important to be in control of the setting.

CHAPTER 3

FOCUS THE CONTENT

In working with thousands of clients for the past five years, from all over the U.S., Canada and Western Europe, one important fact has surfaced. **Anyone will be a better speaker if these three things are present:**

1. FOCUSED CONTENT
2. CORRECT CONTENT
3. COMMITMENT TO CONTENT

We start first with the task of focusing the content. If the content is properly focused, the speaker will be:

- **Clearer**
- **More Concise**

And because the audience will feed back that they're tracking, **the speaker will be less nervous.** Three major benefits from one step - **focusing the content!** This is definitely the place to start.

The method we propose has been dubbed "The Boylan Method." We didn't name it that; our clients did when they called back with their success stories. This isn't just a good idea. **It's a method that has been taught, tried, and proven to be effective.** It was designed after years of research on what's important for a good business presentation. If you want to learn it now, we suggest you actually do the steps as you follow along.

When you <u>hear</u> information, you retain 20%,

When you <u>hear</u> it and <u>see</u> it, you retain 50%,

**If you <u>hear</u> it, <u>see</u> it and <u>do</u> it,
retention goes to 90%.**

So don't just read this — do it step-by-step. Even if you do it only once, you will recall some of the material when you give your next presentation and you will be better.

To begin, think of an upcoming presentation. Remember, presentations aren't always in front of a large group. Many of the most important presentations in business are done one-on-one. Select one you'll be doing soon that can be used for the activities on the next few pages.

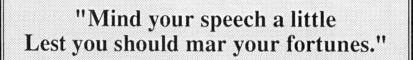

**"Mind your speech a little
Lest you should mar your fortunes."**

William Shakespeare

The first step in preparing content is to answer the following questions. Take time to do it now.

1. Who am I addressing?

    _____
    _____
    _____
    _____
    _____
    _____
    _____

2. What do I want to say?

    _____
    _____
    _____
    _____
    _____
    _____
    _____

3. What are the "benefits" to the listener of what
    I have to say?

    _____
    _____
    _____
    _____
    _____
    _____
    _____

POINT OF VIEW

Defining your Point of View is the most important part of all your preparation. It is the next step. Your Point of View is the single most important idea you want the listener to remember. Notice the word **single**. If your presentation is going to be clear, concise and memorable, you the presenter will have to be absolutely sure you know your own Point of View. When your listeners are asked what you said, this is the sentence they should repeat.

The effect of a Point of View in a presentation can be described by comparing a shotgun to a rifle. The shotgun fires a barrage of pellets, making a messy impression on its target. Isn't it fun when a presentation hits you with a barrage of information? Each audience member makes a decision about which point is most important to remember. The rifle, on the other hand, fires one clean shot with a great deal of concentrated power. A single shot! A single Point of View that hits your listeners with power.

Look back now at how you answered question 2. What is the main idea? Reduce this idea to a simple sentence to create your Point of View. Write it down.

**FOCUS YOUR CONTENT
WITH A
POINT OF VIEW!**

**YOUR POV IS
THE SINGLE
MOST IMPORTANT IDEA
YOU WANT THE LISTENERS
TO REMEMBER!**

The office manager walks into the office of the general manager of the company. He says, *"George, I run word processing. We absolutely must have new equipment in word processing if we are to keep up with the work load. I want to make one point perfectly clear, George, we absolutely must have new equipment in word processing if we want to keep up with the work load."* He continues by giving some facts and benefits that support his clearly stated point of view. He adds a personal story and ends with a recommendation of what kind of equipment to buy. His presentation took only ten minutes but George knows why the office manager walked into his office.

Situational Analysis

People working overtime

Assignments not done

Only one machine

Frustrated staff

Inefficient work conditions

Jobs turned down

Outdated equipment

As a result of the analysis, this was his

POV.

WE MUST HAVE NEW EQUIPMENT if we are to keep up with the work load!

My Point of View is:

_____

_____

_____

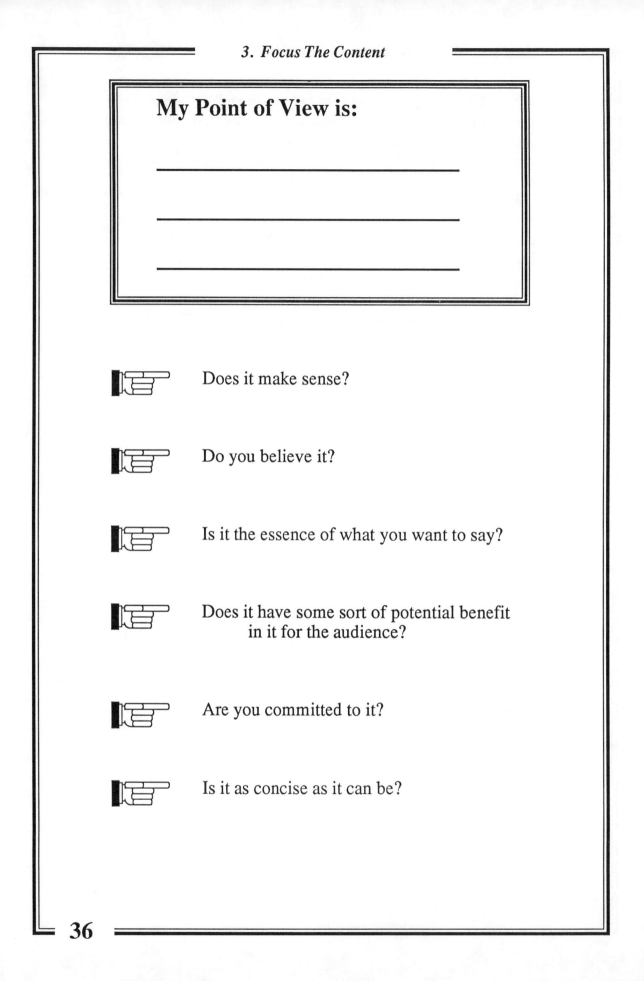

Does it make sense?

Do you believe it?

Is it the essence of what you want to say?

Does it have some sort of potential benefit
in it for the audience?

Are you committed to it?

Is it as concise as it can be?

The point of view can be compared to the tip of an arrow.

If the arrow hits its target broadside, it bounces off, no matter how great an arrow it is. The point of the arrow has to get in to do its job. Once the "point" has entered, the "shaft and feathers" carry the support information. If the point has entered its target, the shaft can even break off, but the arrow will still be effective.

SUMMARY

Writing a point of view takes some thought and training. But it's worth the effort. *It is the single factor that will make all your presentations better.* Once you get the idea of being this clear, you'll be uncomfortable with people who aren't clear. When you've written your Point of View, you will build the body of your presentation by supporting that POV with

1. Benefits
2. Facts
3. Personal Experience

CHAPTER 4

GETTING CORRECT CONTENT

BENEFITS

The point of view determines the rest of the presentation. It is now time to **LIST THE BENEFITS OF THE POV** for the audience. This is your response to their question: "What's in it for me?"

When considering benefits it is important to remember that there are **TWO KINDS OF BENEFITS: EMOTIONAL and LOGICAL.**

Logical Benefits	Emotional Benefits
Money	Recognition
Time	Achievement
Productivity — Efficiency	Security
Improved Product	Pleasure
Safety - Health	Self-Confidence

Marty buys the sports car he's always wanted. His neighbor questions his choice. Marty explains the good mileage, the safety factors and the excellent resale value. He has rationalized his purchase logically. But he really bought the car because he loves it and what it says about his success.

WE MAKE DECISIONS EMOTIONALLY!

The women in the world tend to do this more than men. They call it "using their intuition." There are now seminars and workshops to teach men to be more intuitive managers — to follow their gut-level feelings. We need to trust that intuition when we consider benefits. List emotional benefits as well as logical. Remember, people buy benefits!

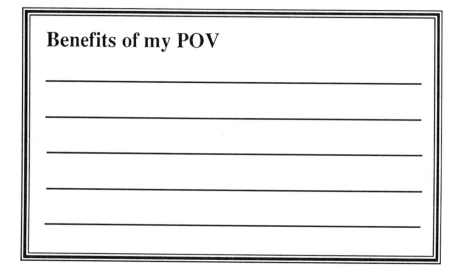

Benefits of my POV

_____

_____

_____

_____

_____

**"A speaker who is attempting to move people
to thought or action
must concern himself with pathos -
i.e., their emotions."**

Rhetoric
by Aristotle

FACTS

The next step is to find the facts that support your point of view. This is the information you got from your research that led you to establish your point of view in the first place.

It is important to give just the facts that are necessary!

Too many presenters think they have to tell everything they know on the subject. They think it adds to their credibility. What it does is presuppose that the listener knows nothing. It also leaves little room for them to direct you to what they want to know through their questions. An important cliche' that works here is:

"Don't try to say everything to everyone at one time."

Facts That Support My Point of View

HAVE YOU EVER FELT YOU WERE GIVEN MORE INFORMATION THAN YOU NEEDED?

Don't bore people with facts they don't need to know.

PERSONAL EXPERIENCE

The audience expects facts when a presentation is given. If you're a good presenter they know you'll talk benefits. They <u>do not</u> expect you to relate to the subject from personal experience.

> *Personal experience is without question*
> *the most powerful content*
> *that you will use.*

When people find out how you personally relate to the subject, they can relate to it too. **This is the part of the presentation that will change you and your audience.** Your voice and your animation come alive when you tell these experiences. It keeps your presentation from becoming flat and boring. Since the content of these stories is your own, you won't be nervous. You won't go blank. The words will come naturally.

Personal experience will make you "you" to the audience. It will allow you to:

- **Be more natural.**

- **Create empathy.**

- **Be real, not plastic.**

Great presenters speak to the heart. **To speak *to* the heart, you have to speak *from* the heart.** The personal experiences help you do that.

There are three types of experiences to draw on for this category.

1. Experiences of your company that tie in.

"Our company has proven how this works. Let me tell you what happened when we did this for another client .... "

2. Experiences of others that you can tell third hand.

"Well, I've never done this, but Gloria has and when Gloria told Frank about it, let me tell you what they said." You start to literally role play that third party conversation. You act out both sides.

3. Your personal stories that relate to your point of view.

"I had an experience that really tells what happens when you use this product ..."

This is sometimes the toughest part because you have to find content that obviously fits the point of view. You can't just tell a story because it's cute. My suggestion is that you start a file of your personal experiences. Begin by listing five things you like to do outside of work that you can tell the whole world about. Write down some experiences you had in each of these activities. Start to categorize these into areas where you can use them.

Let's say, for example, that you're a runner who has run a 10K. In order to get ready for that race, you had to get up a half hour earlier for weeks and run. You are now with a client. Your point of view is that more discipline is needed in handling the inquiries created by the advertising program. They've been slipping through the cracks.

"The most important thing I want you to understand today is this idea of making sure these inquiries are handled. In fact, the discipline needed to make this happen isn't much different than the discipline I have to go through to get ready for a race. Let me tell you what that's all about ..."

Soon you're into the preparation for the race, getting up early, talking about the discipline, the exercise you've got to do. You relate it to what needs to be done by the client to collect the inquiries. You've made it possible and real.

Personal Experience That Relates to Point of View

You have now created what is called in "Speech 101" the body of your presentation. This is the part where you "tell them." *This is getting the "Correct Content."*

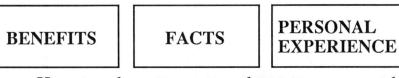

BENEFITS	FACTS	PERSONAL EXPERIENCE

How you choose to arrange them sets your agenda. **The three are totally interchangeable.** The arrangement could be Facts, Personal Experience, Benefits, as long as you don't mix bits and pieces of the categories. You need to decide the order so you can tell your audience where you're going. This is "telling them what you're going to tell them:"

> **Agenda**
>
> 1.
>
> 2.
>
> 3.

After the body comes the time to "tell them what you told them." We call this "Key Points to Remember." This is where you're going for closure. Select two or three main points out of the entire body that you decide are key points. It can be any combination of facts, benefits or experiences. There is only one rule:

No new information is introduced.

Don't surprise the listener with "Oh, and I forgot . . ."

> **Key Points to Remember**
> _____
> _____
> _____

THE RECOMMENDATION

Your final point is your recommendation. This is the specific action you wish to take place that will execute your Point of View.

"As I said, Mr. Client, my Point of View is that you must do marketing research before we're able to position your product. To make this happen, I recommend that you do the study with the XYZ company. It will cost $29,000. It should start May 1 and be completed July 1."

What is the specific action you want to happen that answers the listener's question of "Now What?" The recommendation puts closure on your presentation. **The listeners want and need closure — they expect it.**

My Recommendation Is:

_____

_____

_____

_____

_____

_____

**Make sure the recommendation hooks
directly into your Point of View!**

Some people start their preparation backwards. They actually write their recommendation first and then work backwards. They know exactly what they want to happen and use that to define their Point of View. Whatever works!

POINT OF VIEW OUTLINE

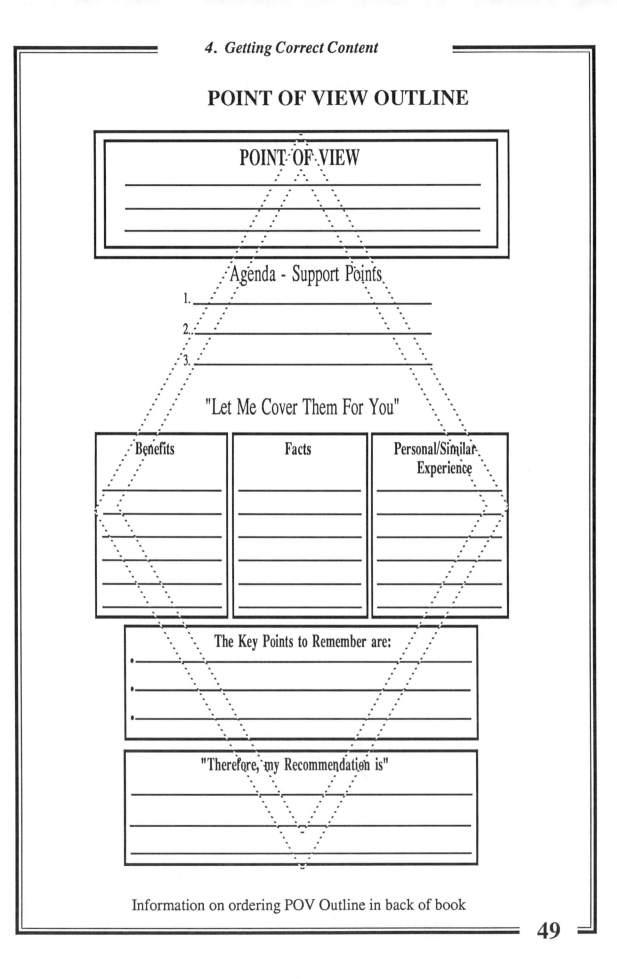

POINT OF VIEW

_____

_____

_____

Agenda - Support Points

1._____

2._____

3._____

"Let Me Cover Them For You"

Benefits	Facts	Personal/Similar Experience
___	___	___
___	___	___
___	___	___
___	___	___

The Key Points to Remember are:

• _____

• _____

• _____

"Therefore, my Recommendation is"

_____

_____

_____

Information on ordering POV Outline in back of book

What you have prepared is the Point of View outline. It is being used by thousands of people across the country to organize successful presentations. It can become your road map for the execution of your presentation.

Notice that there is a diamond on the Point of View outline. It's a reminder to make sure you understand there's a point to the talk.

**You cannot close with a
specific recommendation
if you have no point to close against.**

The diamond also helps you to visualize your presentation mentally. This visualization is called "mind mapping." The mental picture of the diamond will be your map of where to go to next. When this picture is clear in your mind, it will be the visual that will keep you from going blank. It will also keep you from "getting on a roll" and adding a whole other box to the plan. "Oh, and by the way, while I'm up, let me tell you a few more things, talk, talk, talk."

That's why we speak too long. Once we get the adrenalin going we get verbal diarrhea — especially those of us in sales. We're talkers!

The diamond will help you to be more crisp.

Using the Point of View outline will ensure that your Point of View is remembered. The secret is repetition.

As you move from point to point throughout the presentation, make a transition through the Point of View by restating it.

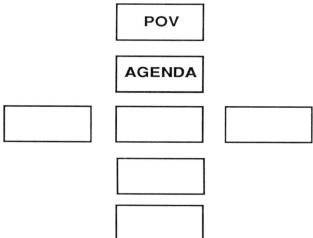

The second thing that happens when you repeat your point of view is:

YOU RE-ENERGIZE YOURSELF

Because you've decided your POV is the most important thing you want them to remember and because you keep saying it . . . .

YOU KEEP FOCUSED

In presenting:

Too often we don't say the *right things*.

We worry too much about saying things *right*.

We've got to worry about saying the *right* things!

Focusing on the Point of View keeps us saying those "right things."

Summary

- My Point of View is:

You have a chance to be an excellent presenter if you have —

1. focused content
2. correct content
3. commitment to your content.

- **Focused content** assures that you'll be:

  - **Centered**
  - **Clear**
  - **Concise**

- **Correct content** means you have selected the pertinent facts that will speak to the listener's needs. The key to making it all more "listenable" is the personal experience. It will make you more real, more natural.

- **Commitment to your content** means you will be interesting, energized and real. Part II will tell you how it will happen naturally without your thinking about it.

A COMPARISON

	Speech 101	**BOYLAN METHOD**	Listener's Agenda
Tell them what you are going to tell them	Introduction	**Review Situation** **Review Needs** **POV Agenda**	What's the point?
Tell them	Body	**Facts** **Restate POV** **Benefits** **Restate POV** **Personal Experience**	What's in it for me?
Tell them what you told them	Close	**Restate POV** **Key Points to Remember** **Recommendation**	Now what?

CHAPTER 5

TO WRITE OR
NOT TO WRITE

Now that you have your organization completed, how do you prepare for the actual presentation? There are three choices:

1. Write it.
2. Memorize it.
3. Speak extemporaneously.

WRITING IT

If you write it all down, you will have thought it through, probably even to the point of editing your own words. These are valid points, but we don't recommend them for several reasons:

 Writing speeches word-for-word takes considerable time and effort.

 Most people have a writing style very different from their speaking style. We tend to use more formal words and sentences when we write.

 The person who writes a script usually is the one who reads it to the audience.

➤ Reading a script usually results in the presenter being boring — a monotone with poor eye contact.

How do you like listening to a presentation that is read to you?

MEMORIZING IT

Some people choose to script their speech and then memorize it. The difficulty with this technique is that the pressures of the actual presentation frequently cause the presenter to go blank. **It isn't a matter of <u>if</u> you'll forget; it's <u>when</u>! Don't try to memorize!**

My mother, besides being a high school physical education teacher all of her life, frequently directed the class play. She loves to tell this story.

One of her students had one line in the class play — only one line, but a critical line. He was to enter stage left and say, "I've been looking all over the place and I can't find Mary."

He rehearsed and rehearsed. He had it perfect. It's opening night. Time arrives for his entrance. On cue, he enters stage left, sees the crowd and for a moment goes blank. He recovers and yells, "I've been looking all over Mary and I can't find the place."

SPEAKING EXTEMPORANEOUSLY

We push the idea of extemporaneous speaking. To the audience, it looks like **casual, confident, organized conversation**. It is not rambling. It is not disorganized. It is not without notes. What is important is where the notes are.

We will talk about the use and production of overhead transparencies in the next chapter. All of our notes, everything we talk about in our seminars, are put on overheads. The transparencies are simple, uncomplicated, and contain very few words. The secret: The notes are on the frames.

Write here what you want to say <u>before</u> you show
   the transparency

TRANSPARENCY

Write here what you want to say <u>after</u> you show
   the transparency

The notes are done on our Macintosh Computer with nice big type. Sheets between transparencies can also contain notes. An actual quotation or verbatim information can be put here to be picked up and read word for word.

IMMERSION PRESENTING

Another way to use notes for extemporaneous speaking is a concept called **immersion presenting**. It's a Walt Disney idea! It's an incredible idea! It's been used in the board rooms of Time/Life, in locker rooms, and on a store window on the Avenue of Americas. It's portable, cheap and it works.

The materials you need are:
- 7 pieces of paper — size depends on your presentation space; e.g., 8-1/2 x 11, layout pads for magic markers, flip charts
- Markers — in a couple of colors
- Masking Tape

Your preparation:

1. On the pieces of paper, write the basic information from your Point-of-View outline, putting material from one block on one sheet. For example, benefits are on one sheet, facts on another.

2. Be sure to label each sheet.

3. Use different colors for titles and underlining. Wake up your creative spirit.

If you are using flip chart paper, use two thicknesses to prevent bleed-through. In pencil, add the notes you'll need to present each sheet. Few participants will notice these notes that will guide you through the presentation..

Fold each sheet in half, securing it with a small loop of masking tape.

IMMERSION

PRESENTING

Ideally, enter the presenting room before your audience does. Using masking tape attach your seven sheets on the available wall space. (We recommend masking tape because it will stick to most surfaces without harm.) **You are ready to give your presentation.**

As you present, unfold your charts. Use the notes to look and sound extemporaneous. When you finish, you'll have a display of visuals that will facilitate retention and questions.

Advantages of Immersion Presenting

Reduces nervous tension

It's cheap

Warms the room — makes it yours

It's portable

Promotes exchange

Presents a focal point for exchange

Increases retention

Creates greater interest

Keeps you going

Shows you're prepared and organized

Can be made for any size space

Makes you more animated

Makes meeting time more efficient

Creates a focal point away from people in a stress situation

Cuts down on misunderstandings

All your visuals are up, showing you have "nothing to hide"

How can you read this and not give it a try?

Immersion presenting! We've got TV people doing it; management people are doing it. How refreshing if you walk into your president's office and he says, "I've got two or three things I want to cover. They're up on the wall. Let's go to work." "Mini-flip charts" work on a wall in anybody's office.

One of our clients went to lunch prepared to present his idea for a $90,000 contract to the marketing director. Lunch passed without discussion of the proposal.   He wasn't worried because they had scheduled time. But as lunch ended, the director said, "Just hand me the proposal. I don't have time to hear it today." Our client followed her out of the restaurant, asking for more time. She refused. He had his seven pieces of paper in his briefcase. He stopped her right where they were — in front of a store on the Avenue of the Americas in New York City — and taped up his charts on a store window. A crowd gathered but he continued. In seven minutes, he had given the essence of his proposal He got the contract. Enthusiasm and focused content sold his proposal. Immersion charts were the technique that helped make it happen.

IMMERSION PRESENTING

Immersion presenting allows for multiple use of audio-visual materials. When a special point needs emphasis, walk over and write it on a flip chart or chalk board. Underline for increased interest. You are now involved in purposeful movement.

SUMMARY

- **Extemporaneous presenting** is planned and organized, with notes on the audio-visual aids, but delivered in a relaxed conversational manner.

- **Extemporaneous presenting** makes movement natural!

- **Extemporaneous presenting** allows each listener, even in a crowded room, to feel as if you are talking directly to him or her.

- **Extemporaneous presenting** gets you out from behind the lectern.

- **Extemporaneous presenting** uses multiple visuals. Preparation of these visuals forces you to be more prepared.

- **Immersion presenting** is an exciting new idea that makes extemporaneous presenting possible.

The Point-of-View outline promotes extemporaneous presenting.

THROW AWAY YOUR SCRIPT
(Listeners will love it.)

SKIP THE MEMORIZING
(Focus on delivery of content, not on memorizing.)

ENJOY THE RELAXED FEELING OF YOUR NEXT ORGANIZED, ENERGETIC, EXTEMPORANEOUS PRESENTATION.
(It's easy with the "mini-flip charts.")

CHAPTER 6

AUDIO-VISUAL AIDS

"One picture is worth a thousand words."
Chinese Proverb

WHY VISUAL AIDS?

Eighty-five percent of everything we learn in life comes from information taken in through our eyes. Only **eleven percent** of what the mind retains comes through our ears. It seems reasonable then that any presentation should be enhanced by the addition of audio-visual materials. Don't forget though,

<u>You</u> are the presentation,
not your visuals.

Audio-visuals are only the extras that will put you ahead of many other presenters. Being alive visually as well as vocally will command more attention.

AV materials help improve your presentation by:

1. Centering the attention of your listeners.

2. Making your ideas easier to understand.

3. Emphasizing your information and ideas.

4. Helping your listeners to remember your talk.

Your choice of AV materials is pre-determined by your content and by the physical set-up of the room you'll be using.

Modern video techniques and slide shows have added new dimensions to the audio-visual world. When you have the preparation time needed, these are excellent tools for a first class presentation.   Most business people are also involved in many impromptu presentations; therefore, we recommend they consider making their own visual aids on a flip chart, a chalkboard or an overhead. The very drawing of the visual during the presentation creates animation that heightens the interest of the listener. Preparation of these aids also adds to your rehearsal time, making you more organized!

POSSIBLE VISUAL AIDS

- Flip charts
- Cards
- Overheads
- Slides
- Video tape
- Video show (a computer-generated slide show on a TV monitor)
- Film
- Product sample
- Demonstrations
- Computer printouts
- Wall charts
- Reports
- "Leave Behind" book
- Props

Do's and Don'ts In Using Visual Aids

☞ Every visual aid should be large, clear, legible, and brief. **If you can't read every word from the back of the room, don't use it.**

☞ Do use color; people respond to color. Try something new: use mega-pens, the oversized magic markers. They are available in most stationery/office supply stores and give you a look a bit out of the ordinary.

☞ Don't rush anything you display. Give everyone time to see and understand the point you are highlighting. Silence at this time is acceptable or read it with them. Don't continue with your presentation until your audience has had time to read the visual.

☞ Each visual should make a single point.

☞ Don't give your talk to your visual aid. Visuals make no decisions; your listeners do. Always face the audience! Glance at the visual to keep your train of thought connected, but talk toward the people.

☞ Never stand in front of what you are showing.

☞ <u>Always</u> test the visual aid ahead of time. If possible, test it in the room where you'll be speaking. Remember O'Toole.

Speakers don't use Murphy's Laws - they use O'Toole's

Murphy said:

"If anything can go wrong, it will."

O'Toole said:

"Murphy was an optimist."

Check out every audio-visual aid. It's part of your responsibility for preparation of the room. Don't assume that because you've ordered what you want it will be there. We have presented in hotels all across the country. We are constantly amazed at how they fail to give us the AV materials we've ordered! We have found that many mistakes can be avoided by using a printed set-up sheet. We have printed the one we use on the following page. Adapt it for your needs.

Remember: No matter how many directions you give,

The presenter has the final responsibility for the room.

SEMINAR ROOM SET-UP

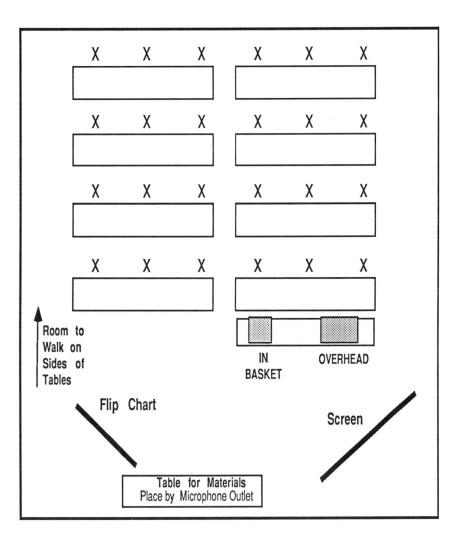

TYPES OF VISUAL AIDS

Our experience with critiquing many presentations has led us to form some very definite opinions on the AV options available. We share them with you with the hope you will think about them as you choose the materials you'll use.

One of the most established and polished forms of AV presenting is the **slide show.** This medium has some very definite pluses and minuses.

+'s	−'s
• Clean and crisp	• Greatly limits flexibility - can't change order
• Controlled	• Eye contact doesn't work in darkened room
• Best way to show pictures	
• Most real	• Worst media to create exchange — too formal
	• Difficult for audience to refocus after viewing slides
	• Dimming room lights can be deadly, especially after a meal.

The usual position of a presenter during a slide show is behind a lighted podium with a written script. This gives off an appearance that is best described as "goulash." It also presents to the listener only one dimension of the presenter - the voice. One dimension makes it difficult to build up an attitude of believability.

There is a definite "don't" involved with slide shows.

Don't let anyone else operate the slides.

No matter how rehearsed the operator, you can be sure there will be a point at which he will get out of sync with the presenter. The repetition of "next slide please" also destroys the flow of the presentation.

Prepared photos, models, and flannel boards are excellent tools. The criteria that determines whether or not they are correct to use is the visibility factor. Can everyone in the room see what you're talking about <u>at the same time</u>? If the answer is no, they are not the correct choice. **Passing an item around is a distraction that takes attention away from you and what you're saying.**

Flipcharts or chalkboards are among the most flexible tools. They are inexpensive and readily available. Plan ahead to emphasize your important words by writing them in bold color with oversized markers. Underline, circle or box with another color for emphasis. Flipcharts can be prepared beforehand. In this case, it is often a good idea to write only on every other sheet to create an unveiling effect, and to prevent the distraction of "see-thru." The value of Immersion Presenting has been discussed in the previous chapter.

Video camcorders are among the newest audio-visual media and undoubtedly one of the most exciting. With these portable machines, it's easy to film people, places, product displays, etc., to play over a TV monitor. It gives the presenter an opportunity to show "how it really is." One of our clients recently won a major account over bigger competitors because he spent an hour interviewing their company's customers with a camcorder.

Props can be described as anything that can accentuate your point. **Use them creatively!** Everyone shows a stack of paper and says, "We did a lot of research." How much more effective if you unveil 40 computer printout sheets taped to the wall when you say it! You've simultaneously added drama as well as an impression of the amount of work done!

A **"Leave-Behind"** is an effective tool many companies use. It is any material you leave for the client to consider, ususaly some form of a proposal summary.

**WARNING: DO NOT HAND OUT
MATERIALS UNTIL YOU ARE FINISHED
OR UNTIL YOU CAN READ THROUGH IT
WITH THE AUDIENCE.**

**Attention will be diverted from you to the
handout.**

The overhead is still the easiest, most workable audio-visual aid. However, it is almost always the most misused. The most common mistake is poorly done overheads, as discussed previously. The second biggest mistake comes in the placement of the screen. <u>The screen belongs in the corner of the room, not in the center.</u> For most people that means the left-hand corner, since this allows them to work at the projector with their right hand.

Overhead
Projector

Speaker

Audience

This placement makes the screen visible to everyone in the room, and the presenter does not have to worry about blocking the image. It also allows the presenter to continually face the audience.

The third error most presenters make when using the overhead is not using the keystone eliminator on the screen. Since the overhead projector is lower than the screen, it will produce an image that is trapezoidal; either the top or bottom will be out of focus, depending on which one you choose to focus. The simple solution is to use the keystone eliminator on the top of the screen.

The overhead transparency requires some special attention. Too many come off the typewriter, through the Xerox machine and are presented with the standard apology, "I know you can't really read what that says, but ...." Don't do it!

If you're going to use overheads, make sure you have the capability to do bar graphs, charts, pictures, and all that good creative stuff.

Some ideas to use when making overhead transparencies:

> **Use a press type machine or a computer to create large, crisp, clean type.**

> **Add color.**

> **Frame each transparency.**

Without a frame, you have no place for notes. Also, without a frame, you've got that irritating white light around everything. If you don't have frames, use masking tape on the glass stage of the overhead to make the opening smaller.

3M has a brand-new product called Pre-Framed Film. It's a transparency with a built-in frame. It's all plastic and equivalent in cost to one with the frame plus the time needed to make it. It's been a staple in our seminars.

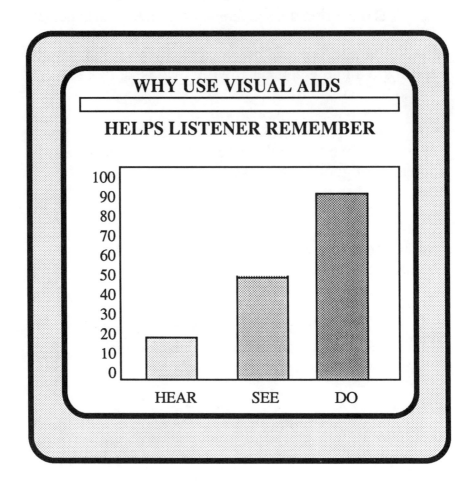

**An Example of an
Effective Overhead Transparency**

Few words

Colored bar graphs

Gives a clear picture

Illustrates one idea

Framed

SUMMARY

<u>SELECT PROPER AV TOOLS</u>

To allow presenter to be:

- Clear

- Energized

- Real

To encourage exchange

To allow the <u>person</u>, not the <u>materials</u>, to be the presentation.

+   +   +   +

And don't forget to select AV materials for all your one-on-one presentations! They can be as simple as one or two cards — or something on the wall. **The Point of View should definitely always be in view.** That's why you walked into the room.

Remember to also use AV materials during small presentations. They can greatly minimize stress that might exist in the room especially during one-on-ones. The issue is no longer between you and the other person. It's out on the table or up on the wall for both parties to focus on. It's much easier to talk about an issue that has been made visible.

Where We've Been

1.   Benefits of presenting skills

2.   **Focused Content** — Audience analysis and preparation of the setting

3.   **Focused Content** — Point of view

     Correct Content — Facts, Benefits, Personal Experience

4.   Extemporaneous Presenting
     Immersion Presenting

5.   Audio visual aids

Where We're Going

1.   Getting **committed to your content.**

2.   Some fine tuning

CHAPTER 7

YOUR DELIVERY SYSTEM

The purpose of this book — the Point of View — is that you will be a better speaker if you have three things:

1. Focused content
2. Correct content
3. Commitment to your content

Part I has described how to make the first two happen.

Most presentation books now talk about "delivery skills needed," which can leave the impression of "training needed here ." After five years of training people to give presentations, it is very evident to me that

**If your Point of View is crystal clear,
and if you have the correct content
(benefits, facts, personal experience),
and if you really are <u>committed</u> to it
You will deliver your presentation with
energy and intensity!**

It's impossible not to! This chapter will emphasize the importance of that energy to the total impact of your presentation. If you really hooked into the first part, the rest will happen!

> **Commitment doesn't necessarily
> make you successful but it does
> make you memorable.
> You need to be remembered
> to be evaluated.**

In business, your success is based on one thing and one thing alone — **your contribution** — not your age, your sex, your college major or even your position. You are always measured by your contribution. We need to communicate that contribution when we speak. To make an even bigger generalization: All these communications are part of our efforts to establish believability.

We are all in the business of "Trust Me."

Research has defined what is needed to establish this trust. An extensive communication project led by Professor Albert Mehrabian was done at the University of California. Many professional presenters like to refer to this study. Three main factors were listed for establishing trust along with their percentage of importance. These three are:

Verbal: The words you say
Vocal: How you sound when you say them
Visual: How you look when you say them

In our seminars we asked clients to rate these by percentage of importance. Few come close to the findings of the communications project.

How important are these three factors
in establishing believability?

Verbal: 7%
Vocal: 38%
Visual: 55%

> **What you say is important,
> but how it's said
> makes the difference.**

Bert Decker, in his program, <u>Speak to Win</u>, makes an analogy to a rocket when he speaks about verbal, vocal, visual.

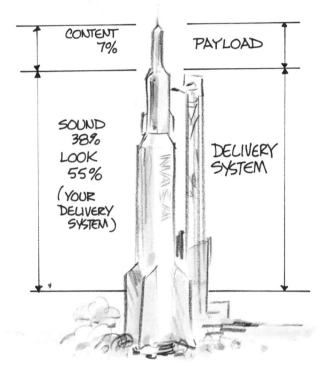

Compare the size of the two parts! The payload is the smaller but more valuable part. It is the reason the rocket is on the launch pad. This can be compared to our **content: the reason you stand up to speak**. But the booster rocket is needed to get the payload off the ground. **If it fails, the valuable payload also fails.**

The booster rocket of your presentation
is your visual and vocal projection — the energy
you put behind your Point of View. Your
commitment to your Point of View — like the
booster — needs to be big.

*How you look and how you sound
tells your audience
you believe you have something
they should hear*.

This doesn't mean you have to look like a drama school graduate. It does mean you have to let the real you come out — the same you that is present when you do one-on-ones. Your energy has to show. It takes energy and animation to convey conviction.

You need to "launch" your point of view! If you don't, it will sit there — go absolutely nowhere! You launch it with energy, with intensity!

Without energy, your idea won't get out of the room. People are indifferent to ideas; they are bombarded with them. The difference comes in how those ideas are presented.

*There is a story about a T.V. newscaster
interviewing the devil.*

*"What is the greatest weapon you use with
people? Is it lies? Jealousy? Hate?"*
*"No! The most successful tool I use is
<u>indifference</u>."*

**Your Energy .. Your Intensity .. will move
your audience out of indifference.**

VISUAL PROJECTION

Within the first 90-120 seconds, people make judgments about a presenter. Your appearance is the largest single factor (58%) that guides that judgment. Do I trust and believe this person?

The most obvious place to begin is posture. What is your position when you stand up to speak? Do drooping shoulders tell the story of how you feel? Developed by habit, those shoulders can give an appearance that suggests low motivation and low self-esteem. A simple exercise can rectify the problem. Pull the shoulders up to your ears. Now put them back as far as they'll go. Now relax. You should find yourself in a position that says, "I'm in charge." This position also makes easier the breath control needed for a well modulated voice.

**Eighty percent of language is unspoken.
It's popularly known as body language.**

Next consider the face. I say, after watching a dead-pan client, **"If you're excited, notify your face."** When we do workshops with our clients, we video-tape them giving eight different presentations. One of the quickest ways to define facial energy is to let the camera zero in on the face and turn off the sound. Start watching faces during meetings, at church, or on TV commercials. It doesn't take long to define why some people are more believable than others.

One of the most frequently asked questions is "What should I do with my hands?" The answer is: **Do the same things you do when you present in the small group**: use those hands for relaxed, normal gestures.

When standing in front of a group, the single most important point to remember about your hands is not to lock them into one position. DON'T GET YOUR HANDS WHERE THEY CAN'T WORK FOR YOU. Some of the favorite positions we see that seem to cause hand paralysis are:

✓	**Praying**	Ala Mother Superior — hands clasped in front
✓	**Parade Rest**	Just like it says — gestures are very difficult from this position
✓	**Hands on Waist**	Looks much more authoritarian than you probably want to appear
✓	**Folded arms in Front**	This is body language that says you've closed yourself off from the world
✓	**Hands in Pocket**	Can become a real distraction, especially if pockets have coins in them
✓	**Fig Leaf**	This is literally a cover-up. Trying to gesture from this position leads to the "fig-leaf flasher."

PRAYING

PARADE REST

HANDS ON WAIST

FOLDED ARMS

HANDS IN POCKETS

THE FIG LEAF

Hands, more than anything else, tell how you're doing. They can really show the butterflies. The hand gestures you use are a sort of voiceless speech. We recommend what is called a **NEUTRAL POSITION**: hands down on the side when you start.

NEUTRAL

When you start in neutral, it's easy to get into the "drive" of gestures.

Practice when you're just standing — not giving a presentation. Watch yourself when you tell a friend your favorite fishing story! A great place to practice is at church. Most people stand with arms folded or in the fig leaf position. Put yours in neutral.

MAKE THE NEUTRAL POSITION A NATURAL POSITION!

Gestures from neutral are natural!

**Some people wish they could leave
their hands and feet
where they are sitting when it's their
turn to stand up and speak.**

LOWER BODY POSTURE IS CONTROLLED PRIMARILY BY WHAT YOU DO WITH YOUR FEET.

To look solidly grounded, put your feet shoulder width apart, toes straight ahead, weight distribution slightly more on the heels. It should give you a feeling of **being centered, balanced, and ready to move forward toward your audience.**

A comparison can be found in the world of architecture. A tall building cannot have a single-level basement. It has to be well grounded or it is in danger of being blown over. Speakers can be "blown over" by challenging questions or a less-than-interested audience. **They need to be visual and present — grounded. This is done by physically taking command of the space.**

Historically, women have been taught a standing position contrary to this, which makes it difficult for them to look like a person in power. It is a position called "hesitation" in modeling — the heel of one foot is brought into the ball of the other, ballet style. Try to stay balanced in that position! Combined with high heels, it usually causes the woman presenter to assume a position called "sinking into the hip." Visually, she appears to be unsteady, backing away from the very audience she wants to impress.

Dress is part of the visual package. The subject has been adequately covered by many good books. But there is one rule to remember. **Dress should be something that works for you - not against you.**

It all adds up to **being committed to your Point of View**. Your content is why you stood up. You have the responsibility to make it **your** content. The presenter always takes precedence over the product. The audience feels the trust, the honesty, and the confidence that is built. If they don't, you've wasted their time and yours.

ARE YOU PRESENT WHEN YOU PRESENT?

THE EYES

Proper eye communication is the single most important visual projection.

When people at our seminars are asked to list the problems they have when presenting, eye contact is invariably mentioned. All the problems heard seem to fit into one of these five categories.

EYE-COMMUNICATION PROBLEMS

- Reading the presentation

- Looking at shoes, ceiling, visuals

- Looking over people's heads

- Eye dart — looking at everyone

- Looking at same few people all the time

One or all of these give the listeners a message that says you are not confident, you are not <u>committed</u> to your POV. They also say you don't care if you have any impact.

**If your eyes say you don't believe
what you're saying,
why should the listener believe it?**

What if your boss came into your office, sat down and started talking. *"I just wanted to talk to you a little bit about how well you've been doing. As head of the accounting area, you have done a good job in earning the respect of your people. Your people work for you."* You like what you're hearing but you can't help noticing he hasn't yet engaged your eyes. *"I've looked at the reports you've turned out, and they're really good. When we do our next review, I think we can reward all this hard work. But I just wanted to stop and tell you how I felt — nice talking to you."* He leaves. The words were terrific, but he never looked at you. How do you feel?

We do this exercise in our seminars. The most frequent answers are:

"Didn't feel he had confidence in himself."

"Didn't believe him."

"Got confused — didn't really know what he thinks."

"Felt very uncomfortable — for him and for me."

"Don't care what he thinks if he won't look at me."

"Didn't trust him!"

How do you feel when a person
who is talking to you
doesn't look you in the eye?

There are some tricks to make eye contact easy to learn. The easiest is to picture your audience as the individuals they are and choose to talk to them one at a time. Look right at one person, and

HAVE A 5-SECOND MINI-CONVERSATION WITH HIM OR HER!

Talking to one person is easy. You do it all the time in your one-on-one presentations. Why should anyone be nervous talking to just one person? All the people in the room will hear you, but you are talking to only one at a time.

> # The whole presentation should be a series of 5-second mini-conversations.

The second, but most important directive, is to make sure you

BUY YOUR OWN IDEA!

If you are focused and have the right content, it will be natural to talk about it to one person, and your energy will be there.

The Eye — pathway to the heart

BENEFITS OF 5-SECOND EYE COMMUNICATION

☞ Tells audience you are confident

☞ Relaxes you — gives you a
   one-on-one feeling

☞ Generates more interest

☞ Promotes conversational style —
   not presentational

☞ Helps delivery skills work naturally
   Gestures
   Vocal variety
   Movement

"To involve a person, you must
speak to his eyes."

Napoleon

When the group is small — under 40 — make an effort to engage each person's eyes at least once if time allows. When the group is large, mentally divide the crowd into blocks. Select one person in each block to be the object of your focus. This direct focus at such a distance creates an impression of individual eye contact with most people in the focused area.

The most frequent mistake made with eye contact in small groups is to zero in on the key decision maker. For most, this "spotlight position" becomes uncomfortable, and leads to a negative reaction that has little to do with the spoken words. It also leaves the rest of the people feeling neglected and unimportant.

Looking into listener's eyes has another advantage for speakers. It gives them instant feedback. Just as in any personal conversation, the eyes will tell whether or not the listener is connecting to what is being said. This feedback can be the incentive the speaker needs to become even more committed to the presentation.

> # You listen to the audience
> # with your eyes.

Lou Tice, a famous self-image psychologist, speaks about a principle called <u>self-talk</u> that I think is important to mention here. He says we all talk to ourselves 800 words a minute every moment we're awake our entire life so everyone who is physically in front of you during a presentation isn't necessarily really there. Their self-talk can be more captivating than your talk. As the presenter, you need to keep these people in the room ... or see if they have left. The way you do it is with eye contact.

One final comment on eye contact: consider the feeling that comes when someone is avoiding your eyes. The impression almost always is one of distrust - a negative impact to any presentation.

WHEN A PRESENTER HAS POOR EYE COMMUNICATION, IT SAYS:

"REGARDLESS OF WHAT YOU SEE, I AM REALLY NOT HERE."

The importance of being present with your eyes was brought home by an incident with my son. Steve, a goalie for the high school hockey team, came in after the game. I was in my chair reading the newspaper. The conversation went something like this.

"Hi, Dad. We won."

"Great, Steve. What was score?"
        (Not looking up from the paper)

"Three to two."

"Must have been a good game."
        (Still reading)

"It really was, Dad."

"How many saves did you have, Steve?"
        (Still reading)

"Thirty-six."

"Man, you were busy. (Still reading)
When's the next game, Steve? Steve?"

Steve left. Why? Because I was never there. Not there!

**YOU ARE THERE WITH YOUR EYES
OR
YOU'RE NOT THERE!**

And so we need 5-second eye contact. We need to have extended eye communication or we're just not there!

Three Levels of Eye Contact

Intimacy
Intimidation
Involvement

We know what **intimacy** is all about. When we're in love, we don't have to say anything. We can talk with our eyes.

Intimidation can be described as a strong stare. It looks right through you. That's not what you want in a presentation. Your audience is immediately put into a defensive position.

The goal in eye communication is called **involvement**. It's the communication that says, "You are important to me."

Eye communication completes what is called visual projection. Along with your **body position** and your **voice,** it is the medium that will communicate your commitment to your Point of View. Your nervousness will be controlled. You will be perceived as a clear, concise presenter. The competence you have will come through.

Commitment to your Point of View will allow you to look people in the eye — to converse with them with clarity and intensity. You will communicate!

VOCAL PROJECTION

It is a strong consensus among psychologists that the voice is second only to eyes in influencing others. In the rating of importance for believability, vocal was given 38% — seventeen points higher than the importance of the actual words. **The question then is — how do you sound when you stand up to present?**

One fact is certain:

**If your Point of View is crystal clear
and if you are <u>committed</u> to it,
you will have an energy, an intensity,
that will be transmitted into
vocal energy *naturally*.**

Showing this excitement through your voice is important to develop trust and believability.

The main sound producers for humans are the vocal cords, small bands of tissue that stretch across the voice box (larynx). When we speak, we pull the vocal cords by their attached muscles, narrowing the opening. Air coming from the lungs through the larynx vibrates the cords and we speak. The tighter the cords, the higher the sound. Conversely, the more relaxed the cords, the lower the sound. General muscle tension caused by the nervousness of the presentation moment can be very noticeable to the audience through the voice. The high-strung tones that result are as difficult to listen to as the monotone.

Most complaints about the voice center around these qualities:

Pitch
Inflection
Emphasis
Vocal Resonance

Pitch refers to the highs and lows of the voice. The voice should move like a roller coaster, going up and down to create interest. Compare the movement of your voice in a two-syllable word versus a three-syllable word.

Tragic
Commotion

Let it be natural, not imposed. A lack of pitch results in a monotone. An overuse of pitch is also distracting. The frequent modulation of the fashion commentator's voice does not belong in a business presentation.

Inflection is the way we change the pitch of our voice by the emotion put behind the words. Compare the different effects of the sentence "Turn out the light" when said with anger, with friendliness, and then with seduction.

Particularily watch the inflection you use at the end of sentences. Being flat at the end is regarded as authoritative, the voice used when giving orders. The more preferred method for presenters is to pitch the voice down at the end of a sentence. It is the technique used by national newscasters. Going up makes each sentence a question and is regarded as giving away power or seeking approval.

Emphasis refers to choosing the words you want to stand out. Try saying "What voice makes you react?" five times, putting emphasis on a different word each time.

"**What** voice makes you react?"
"What **voice** makes you react?"
"What voice **makes** you react?"
"What voice makes **you** react?"
"What voice makes you **react?**"

Vocal resonance refers to the richness of the voice. In today's world, lower is regarded as more pleasant. Since vocalization is a muscular activity, it is possible to change a voice. Getting a lower quality can be achieved by putting a pen in your mouth, biting it with your teeth, and talking aloud. Your voice will automatically be lowered. Consistent use of this exercise will lead to a permanently deeper voice.

Improving breath control is one of the easiest ways to improve the voice. Breathing from the diaphragm with deep breaths will produce a calming, more resonant voice. A simple way to practice is to read the newspaper aloud as if you were a national newscaster. Open your mouth to at least the size of a half dollar when speaking. This will help eliminate nasality and improve articulation. Pace your reading — speed up or slow down for emphasis.

If you have a tape recorder, use it. Remember, when you play it back, what you hear is more like the voice other people hear than what you hear. The cavities in our skull give us a distorted perception of how we sound.

TO IMPROVE YOUR VOICE, TAPE RECORD IT, LISTEN TO IT, THEN FIX IT!

When you listen to the tape of yourself speaking, count your non-words. The use of non-words — "er" — "ah" — "ummm" — is a vocal habit attributed partially to nervousness. These words, which become quite habitual, usually come from a fear of silence. Speakers put them in to fill the quiet while they're pausing to think. Elimination of these non-words is a natural by-product of developing and practicing new speaking skills. When the speaker is organized and rehearsed, confidence is up. The speaker knows where the presentation is going. A bit of silence is an addition, not a distraction. It actually gives you authority.

Non-words have an adverse affect on the audience as well. They create a mood of boredom. The listeners become tired of waiting for a message that is hidden between repeated ah's, umm's, or "you know's." It's unfortunate that boring is the adjective given to so many "in-house" meetings because non-words were spoken more than words. Use your POV: Know where you're going!

> *There is the story of the dull-looking man*
> *who said to the bartender,*
> *"Make me a zombie!"*
> *The answer: "I can't ...*
> *God beat me to it!"*

> **"There is no index of character**
> **so sure as the voice."**
> **Disraeli**

Commitment to your POV will change how you sound. If <u>you</u> don't <u>sound</u> like you bought your own idea, why should anyone else?

SUMMARY

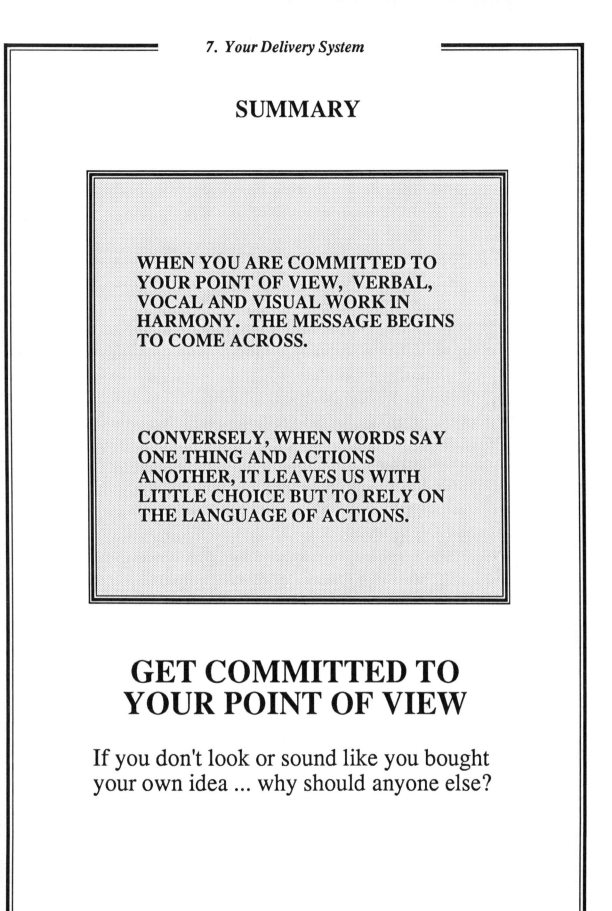

WHEN YOU ARE COMMITTED TO YOUR POINT OF VIEW, VERBAL, VOCAL AND VISUAL WORK IN HARMONY. THE MESSAGE BEGINS TO COME ACROSS.

CONVERSELY, WHEN WORDS SAY ONE THING AND ACTIONS ANOTHER, IT LEAVES US WITH LITTLE CHOICE BUT TO RELY ON THE LANGUAGE OF ACTIONS.

GET COMMITTED TO YOUR POINT OF VIEW

If you don't look or sound like you bought your own idea ... why should anyone else?

CHAPTER 8

NERVOUS?

The first problems of presenting brought up by most clients is **nervousness.**

Nervousness is felt and occasionally it is paralyzing. It is very real.

IF IT IS NOT OVERCOME, ALL ELSE WILL FAIL.

KEYS TO OVERCOMING NERVOUSNESS

1. Focused Point of View

2. Commitment to Point of View

3. Transitions through Point of View

Everyone, no matter how experienced, suffers from nervousness. The secret is what you do with it. Every coach knows that nervous tension is a good thing if you put it to work for you. It gets the adrenalin flowing! Nervousness can be lessened for you if you know how.

Your point of view is the primary key to reducing nervousness. It focuses your knowledge, and knowledge builds confidence! If you are committed to this Point of View, there'll be no need to stammer for words — you'll speak from your commitment. When you believe what you're saying is important, it is natural to think alive and then act alive.

"KNOWLEDGE IS POWER"

The Point of View outline also is a tool for reducing nervousness. After you've written, it's almost impossible not to visualize it mentally. Seeing the actual diamond shape always lets you know where you're going next. No need to panic that you'll get lost.

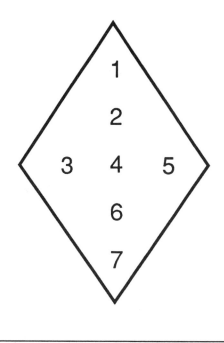

REHEARSAL

The ultimate factor in reducing nervousness and building confidence is rehearsal. We can't say it loudly enough!

IF YOU

DON'T

REHEARSE,

DON'T

PRESENT!

MENTAL VISUALIZATION

No matter what your title is or how small the presentation is, rehearsal is an absolute necessity. This can take many forms. Mental visualization of your presentation is probably the simplest. It requires no special space or practice audience. **Visualization is a key skill of peak performers**. They have pictured how they will move through the presentation. They have programmed themselves for success.

Visualization is important to reduce nervousness.

If you are going to be part of a team presentation, it is vital that you rehearse as a team. Establish your agenda and the time allotment for each person. Any team presentation is usually a major opportunity for your department, your company and you. It is critical then that everything work as well as it's expected. So be tough on yourself and other members of your team. In preparation for the exchange time, each presenter should prepare at least five questions that likely will be asked. Let the team members critique the answers.

Rehearsal will give you answers to all your questions. Having answers adds to your confidence, further reducing your nervousness.

Rehearse:

[ ] in actual room

[ ] with all participants

[ ] with all visual aids

[ ] with full effort — check timing

[ ] to assure all responsibilities are assigned

A critique is a part of any presentation but an absolute necessity for rehearsal if you want to reduce nervousness. This one is simple and covers all the critical points. Be sure you also include it as part of your team preparation .

CRITIQUE

 A must in rehearsal

 A must after presentation

	GOOD	AVERAGE	NEEDS TO IMPROVE
[ ] Clarity of POV			
[ ] Organization of thought			
[ ] Did visual aids help and work as planned			
[ ] Energy level...intensity... toward POV			
[ ] Eye contact...5-sec eye bursts			
[ ] Voice ... loud enough, "energizing", articulate			
[ ] Listener involvement... "exchange"			
[ ] "Did you use this opportunity ...to SHINE?			

PHYSICAL AIDS

Proper breathing is a physical factor in controlling tension. It's a technique well known by professional athletes. They can increase or decrease their heartbeat at will by changing their breathing patterns.

1. Place your hands at the bottom of your rib cage on the diaphragm.

2. Take a deep breath, feeling the diaphragm expand.

3. Slowly push the diaphragm to exhale.

Take five to six deep breaths with your diaphragm. You'll lower your metabolism ... and relax. This deep breathing will reduce perspiration, calm you and get you centered. Use it right before it's your turn to go on.

Some quick exercise will also help reduce the physical tension. A brisk walk around the block or a few toe touches are stimuli to deep breathing. Do isometric exercises in your chair 60 seconds before you speak. This will increase your circulation and bring more oxygen to your brain. You'll be more alert and tend to go blank less. A silent prayer is also calming as well as soft music. **But absolutely nothing surpasses proper preparation.**

Your Goal:

Peak Performance under Peak Pressure

***There is nothing wrong with
butterflies!***

***You just have to get them to fly
in formation!***

Bert Decker

SUMMARY

- Nervousness is not bad. It just must be controlled for a good presentation.

- The Point of View provides the important key for overcoming nervousness.

- The Point of View outline provides a road map for the presentation.

- Rehearsing is an absolute necessity.

- Mental visualization is a skill that controls nervousness.

- Physical steps can be taken to reduce the tension.

CHAPTER 9

BEGINNINGS AND ENDINGS

Organization of the beginning and ending of your presentation has been established with the POV outline. You begin with your Point of View and end with your recommendation. Because of the importance of the two parts, some special tips can be given.

BEGINNING

The beginning has to grab the interest of the audience. More than any other part of the presentation every detail has to be planned. The cruel realization is

You can never take back a first impression!

The audience makes a decision about you in the first two minutes. Preparation can assure it will be a positive one.

There are several suggestions on beginnings that have a twofold purpose of grabbing the audience and relaxing the speaker.

1.   <u>Tell a story</u> - people love to hear stories, especially personal ones. Your familiarity with the story will make the words come easily.

2.   <u>Ask a good question</u> - This can be used to arouse curiosity as well as involve the audience. "How many of you can remember your first car?" A second or third question establishes a level of familiar comfort in the room. The people have become involved with what you're saying.

3.　　Make a statement that cements mutual interest between you and your listeners. Don't use the word "I" in this opening statement. It can leave the impression you are talking "at" them. "All of us are in this room tonight because we are parents — we are parents concerned about the alcohol problem in our high school."

There are also a couple of "Don'ts"

1.　　Don't start with all the usual platitudes. "I'm so happy to be in front of this really great group in this fantastic town." People don't always believe these and they can begin an attitude of distrust.

2.　　Don't give a long introduction to your topic. People do not need or want the entire history of your subject. If you grab them with what you have to say, they'll ask for more.

3.　　Don't use <u>any</u> kind of notes for the first minute.

This is definitely the time to focus on the eyes of the audience. Be present!

There are some physical preparations you can make to assure your beginning will get you off the launch pad.

1. Practice walking from where you're going to sit to where you're going to speak. Visualize arriving in front of the group. What do they look like? What does it feel like?

2. Decide which people you are going to have a 5-second eye communication with. Make a definite decision who will be number one, two and three. When you have a mini-conversation with each of these three people, you will be "off and running" into a relaxed, confident presentation.

If it is a large group make sure you select three people in different parts of the group.

3.   Practice standing in perfect posture and just being present for a moment. Entertainers are terrific at this! They come up and soak in the audience. They "arrive". Have the ability to be present!

ENDING

> *"Never rise to speak*
> *'til you have something to say;*
> *and when you've said it, cease."*
> *Calvin Coolidge*

People need a sense of closure. They want the ends tied up in a neat package.   It is called the "Gestalt theory of closure." The audience wants an answer to their "now what?" A review of key points and your recommendation will do this.

The impact of your ending can be increased with a memorable statement. Collect and catalogue these statements when you find them so they are readily available. One of the favorites we use is:

"May you prosper to the same extent
your customers do as a direct result of your
value to them."

Christopher Haggerty

SUMMARY

- Beginnings and endings are peak attention time for the audience and merit special preparation.

- Audience contact must be established at the beginning. There are several suggested ways to make this happen.

- Part of the preparation for the beginning involves a physical rehearsal.

- Audiences need and expect closure. They want to know "now what?"

CHAPTER 10

HUMOR?

Humor is always an issue when people talk about giving presentations. How? When? And what jokes? Looking for these answers can be another source of nervous tension for presenters.

The purpose of a business person in a presentation is to communicate content. Unless you are invited to be the "after-dinner" speaker, you are not present to entertain. <u>Getting belly laughs is not your job!</u> You are there to make your point in the most interesting way possible.

TELL YOUR STORIES

Humor can be achieved naturally when you are you! <u>You will be real when you tell your own stories.</u>

**Your own stories are where
you should look for humor!**

Book stores have shelves of joke books for every kind of presenting situation.

Don't buy them! They put you out of character! They are <u>not your stories,</u> which means they will be:
1. Difficult to remember
2. Clumsy to tell

Create your own book of stories - create your own anthology! It will take more time but these <u>are your stories</u>! You'll never forget them!

Take your work seriously!
Take yourself less seriously!

In the chapter on content, several ways were suggested for gathering your personal stories. Begin now to record your stories and to TRUST THEM! They will give you the opportunity to laugh at life and at yourself. And when you laugh, you won't be alone. Your stories will add humor to your presentations.

Have you ever told a joke
and had it fall dead?
Personal stories won't crash!

On the same plane with jokes that crash are jokes that are just thrown in without any connection to what's going on. You won't worry about the response or misplacement because your stories will be chosen to drive home the POV. They won't bomb! There is *NO RISK* involved in stories that are your own.

Another important advantage of personal stories - even when they're funny - is that they build the feeling of *TRUST ME!* Your co-workers and employees will see you in a new light when your stories say, "I've been where you are!" Some of your failures might even be revealed which definitely puts you in the realm of the real!

We are all our own biggest joke!

Recently I was eating breakfast in a hotel where I was giving a presentation. I was sure my normal, cheery disposition was also present. A conversation with the lady at the next table revealed that there was a major medical seminar going on in the hotel. When she asked why I was there I said, "I'm giving a presentation." Before I could say more she said, "Oh, I know, you must be the person talking on depression, right?"

Places To Look For Your Own Humorous Stories

1. Your vacation stories

2. Your family

3. Growing-up years

4. Your fears

5. When you were just beginning

6. Car stories

7. Pets and other animals

8. Little children

9. Church-related stories

10. Moments of great triumphs

11. Your hobbies

12. Your job

SUMMARY

- Humor in presentations should be natural — a part of the total story.

- The best sources of humor are your own stories that fit into the presentation.

CHAPTER 11

QUESTION-AND-ANSWER TIME

It's a fact! People begin to "buy" when they start asking questions. If so many people know that, why is the question and answer time left up for grabs? Why is it usually just tacked on to whatever time is left after the presentation?

AGENDIZE FOR EXCHANGE

I call the question and answer time - exchange time. It's obviously important because this is where the "selling" takes place and that's the reason you gave the presentation. It was one of my truly big BGOs that this special time cannot be left to chance. It has to be planned! I call it THE EXCHANGE AGENDA.

Johnny, 7 years old, comes to his mother and says, "Where did I come from?"

The mother gulps and asks, "What did you say?"

Johnny repeats "Where did I come from?"

The mother is ready this time. "Well, it's about time you ask that question. Dad and I have been thinking you would. You see, Johnny, your dad and mom love each other a lot. Because of that, we sometimes lie close to each other and something called a sperm passed between Daddy and Mommy. It happened about 8 years ago and you were conceived. You started to grow in Mommy's tummy and Mommy's tummy got bigger every month. I went to see Dr. Brown. He checked my tummy every month to make sure you were growing okay. My tummy got bigger and bigger for 9 months. And then I went to the hospital. Daddy and Dr. Brown were there. Johnny, you know where you came from? You came out of Mommy's tummy - that's where you came from!"

Johnny's face was one of great puzzlement. "Wow!" he said. "That's the most incredible story I've ever heard. Frank, my friend, comes from Boston and I was just wondering where I came from!"

Have you ever been at a presentation where you've gotten more than you needed to know? The Exchange Agenda eliminates that.

THE EXCHANGE AGENDA

This is how this agenda is set up:

1. Take the total amount of time allowed for the presentation. Divide this number by 3.

   Example: 90 minutes has been given to you. 1/3 of 90 = 30 minutes

2. Plan on 30 minutes of actual presentation time. If you work with a team, this is the <u>total</u> time the team can use. Using the Point of View outline will make sure you get maximum use of this time.

3. At the end of 30 minutes, give a <u>visual</u> summary of what was said. This will give the audience a <u>focus</u> for their questions.

4. Use the remaining 2/3 of the time for discussion. Open up the session for questions. Use the time to HEAR AND ANSWER THE NEEDS OF THE AUDIENCE.

5. During the last 10% of the time of the discussion time, summarize, make your recommendation and close.

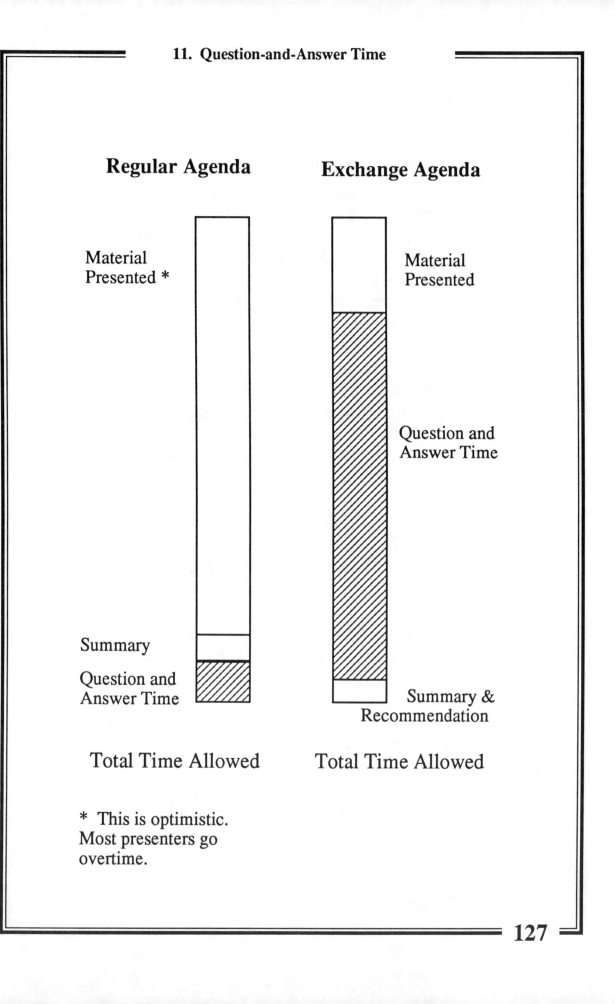

Regular Agenda

Material
Presented *

Summary

Question and
Answer Time

Total Time Allowed

* This is optimistic.
Most presenters go
overtime.

Exchange Agenda

Material
Presented

Question and
Answer Time

Summary &
Recommendation

Total Time Allowed

BENEFITS OF EXCHANGE AGENDA

1. **It builds believability.** Have you ever listened to a really smooth presenter and felt disbelief? It's not that you don't trust him/her. You just want to know if that person is real. Opening yourself to questions gives your audience a chance to see how real you are. People ultimately "buy" people, not ideas.

2. If you're presenting for a new piece of business along with competitors, **the Exchange Agenda will differentiate you from the others.** Yours will be the presentation that will allow the buyer to talk.

3. **Talking gives listeners the opportunity to clarify what they want** so the presenter can focus on the information needed.

4. **Exchange allows a chemistry to happen** between the audience and the presenter. Chemistry has to develop to sell.

5. **Questions are focused** so the listeners gets the whole story.

6. **A feeling of trust develops.** Listeners feel you haven't held anything back.

7. **Actual presentation time is short.**
   Listeners can grasp the entire presentation
   while listening energy is high.

8. Less actual presenting time makes **the
   presenter less nervous.** Questions allow
   time to just "talk about it".

9. **The presenter gets immediate feedback.**
   Objections and questions can be handled in
   person, not after you've left.
   Misconceptions or misunderstandings of
   your material can be clarified immediately.

10. **Exchange agenda follows classic sale's
    training.** "You'll never know how you're
    doing until the prospect is allowed to talk."

11. Used at internal meetings, **this agenda
    allows employees to participate,** to
    contribute, to be visible .... and therefore
    valued.

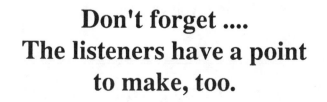

**Don't forget ....
The listeners have a point
to make, too.**

The idea of "sitting down" after using only a third of the planned time strikes fear in the hearts of most sellers. They feel they have to talk more to give the audience what they think it needs to know. The simple truth is:

**Only when you ask "what do you think?"
will you really find out exactly what they want.**

You will then be using two-thirds of your time addressing the <u>real needs of the listeners</u>.

- This agenda takes courage!
- This agenda breaks the mold of what's been done!
- This agenda works! Excited clients tell us it does!
- The way you will make it work is by doing it.

 This agenda demands that you know your material. Questions will quickly reveal those who do not have a grasp of their subject.

Many people are capable of giving a slick presentation. I have a daughter — Susan — who's a commercial physical education major at Colorado State. She has the gift of presence. She's attractive and articulate. She knows how to present. I know if you gave her an outline of a subject, she could deliver a good presentation just from that information. One thing though, don't ask her any questions when she's finished because she won't really know the subject. That's the point! People know you know your stuff when you can answer their questions. Your answers will show you've done your work!

**If you don't know your material,
don't use this agenda!**

The major fear with the exchange agenda — in fact, with most question and answer sessions — is
"What if they just sit there?"
There are some things you can do to make sure they don't.

First of all — Set them up. When you begin, tell them what you are going to do.

> "I know there's going to be a lot of discussion on this subject, so today I'm going to give you the essence of the idea. Your questions will determine which details you want to hear."

Then — Prime the Pump. Have at least four questions prepared for you to ask along with the answers.

But — Don't forget to be quiet — Silence is a great stimulus. Let it happen!

HANDLING QUESTIONS

When the questions start, there are several things you can do to keep control of the situation.

1. If someone's hand goes up immediately, it's a good idea to go to someone else, if possible. If there is going to be an antagonistic question, this is most likely to be the one. By going to the other person first, you help take the "wind out of the sails."

2. Listen closely for the concept in the question. Find the issue!

3. Do not repeat the question unless it wasn't heard by the audience and then repeat it exactly. Do not rephrase it to your advantage. This can build a feeling of distrust.

4. Don't say "Good question." If you don't repeat that phrase for each question, the implication is that some questions aren't good.

5. When you answer the question, be sure to tie the answer back to your Point of View.

6. Use your visuals! Point to them, touch them, use them for your answers. Let the notes you have on them keep you focused and in charge.

7. Don't forget your humor. An attitude of lightness will encourage more questions.

8. Make your answers brief and to the point. This is not the time for another presentation.

9. Don't let an answer turn into an argument. Arguing will only make you look out of control. There are techniques to handle hostile questions.

10. Don't change from your presentation style. This will only confuse your audience and lead to a feeling of distrust.

QUESTIONS LET YOUR AUDIENCE

KNOW YOU THINK THEY'RE

IMPORTANT!

There are also some physical recommendations to be made about handling questions.

1. Raise your hand and step toward the audience while saying something like, "Before I summarize, are there any questions?" Too many presenters step back at this point, fold their arms and ask defensively, "Any questions?" They appear ready to fend off an attack. Your body language must say you really want questions.

2. When you complete the answer, be sure you are looking at someone other than the person who asked the question. This will help eliminate the problem of one person dominating the questions.

3. If you raise your hand as you complete your answer, it will be a signal that you are ready for another question.

4. When you answer a hostile question, end physically away from the person, not looking at him and not asking, "Does that answer your question?"

Consider yourself a researcher when you are asking questions. This stance means you do not have all the answers but are open to receiving more information. This can be extremely helpful in handling the antagonistic listener. An example: You've just given a presentation recommending television be used as part of the advertising budget. During the exchange one of the listeners says hostilely, "TV is overused. I don't like money being spent on TV."

You respond, "I thought TV might be a touchy issue. What do the rest of you think?"

When you poll your audience, one of two things will happen, both to your favor.

1) They will <u>disagree</u> with the challenge. They have now taken your side and will support you against further challenges from that listener.

2) They will <u>agree</u> with the challenge. As a researcher you have now been given a valuable piece of information. Use it! Let them know you've heard them and you'll be the winner.

Remember: **The presenter is the lead person in the room but not the only brain in the room.**

Above all, learn to be an active listener when dealing with questions, especially the hostile ones. Frequently the words spoken are just a mask for the real issue. It is your job as the presenter to bring out what you believe is the issue behind the question. If you don't, there will be a hidden agenda in the room working contrary to your agenda.

Remember, too, that you are in control. It is your job to end the questions. This can be according to your planned time agenda or sooner. If the question time is becoming destructive time, terminate it, but don't forget your ending.

Most presenters know that the greatest retention for the listener occurs at the beginning and the end of the presentation. Since the ending will be remembered,

Don't let someone else's question end your presentation!

When the question and answer time is completed,

Don't forget to summarize!

Following your Point of View outline, summarize the facts, benefits and experiences. Most importantly, restate your Point of View. If something a questioner said fits your purpose, use it for support. If you have successfully used the exchange agenda, you will be on new ground with your audience. They will have developed more trust in you and you will be aware of it. It will be second nature to make an impact with your ending.

SUMMARY

- The question-and-answer time is such an important part of the presentation that it must be planned.

- The exchange agenda is a new idea that makes maximum use of the question-and-answer time.

- The exchange agenda has incredible benefits for both the speaker and the audience.

- The speaker can take definite steps to be in control of the question session.

- Hostile questions can be handled to the advantage of the speaker if the speaker takes the position of a researcher.

- Question-and-answer sessions need to end with your summary.

CHAPTER 12

IF YOU SPEAK A LOT

Some of you are in jobs that require you to give a lot of presentations. This chapter is for you! The years of giving seminars have given me the opportunity to learn some techniques that you might find as useful as I do.

PREPARATION

 Draw a diagram for a room set-up that is just the way you want it. At the bottom list exactly what you want in the room. Keep copies of this diagram on hand. Send one to the place where you'll be speaking at least two weeks before the engagement. Hotel staff continually tell me we are one of the few companies that do this simple step that makes their job so much easier. (The form we use is on page 65.)

 Keep the mega-pens, overhead pens — all needed supplies in a little bag always ready to go. Cosmetic kits are great for this. They're small and plastic lined.

 Purchase a small time clock to pack in your necessity bag. Set it in the front where you can see it easily. A speaker should never check their watch. It is an impetus for everyone in the audience to check theirs. To make sure you don't check yours out of habit, it is best to remove your watch before you start. The visible clock will let you know you are on schedule.

 File your overhead tranparencies in manila file folders labelled according to subject categories. Number the folders in order of the usual subject sequence. Number the transparencies within the file.

This system has several benefits. When the file folders are labelled by topic, it facilitates flexibility in your presentation. The sequence of materials can be changed without any noticable disruption. There is no need to shuffle through a huge pile of transparencies to find the ones you want if you change from your original plan. It also makes it easy to refer back to your visuals during the question and answer session.

Numbers and labels lend themselves to a quick, easy clean up. If necessary, someone other than you can put them back into proper order.

 If you use a substantial amount of hand out material, have it sent to the hotel — at least two weeks before you arrive. This circumvents the growing problem of airline luggage not arriving at its destination on time. On the label be sure to put SAVE AT REGISTRATION DESK FOR GUEST (your name) ARRIVING ON (date). LATE ARRIVAL. It is a good idea to put the words "Registration Desk" more than once on the top of the box. It is not easy to find a box of materials that gets lost in a large hotel.

- **IMPORTANT** — Always carry your presentation materials with you. They are too important to risk having them not show up. I always keep copies of all handout materials with me. If necessary, they could be reproduced at the place of the presentation.

Assume total responsibility for the room whether or not it's in-house. Find out before hand how to control the temperature. Determine the path of entrance by closing some doors. (This is especially important if you anticipate latecomers.) On the flip chart write "No Smoking" or carry signs to designate smoking tables.

Make every effort to look at the room the night before you speak (even if it's late after a plane ride). It gives you the security to know all is in place, and most importantly it allows you to visualize the room. Visualization is an outstanding method of rehearsal. People who speak a lot use this method extensively to mentally prepare.

 If calling people by name is important to you, take along a supply of 4'x 6' index cards and marking pens. Each person can quickly make an easily readable nameplate by folding the card in half and placing it on the table in front of them.

 Color coordinate your wardrobe to simplify packing. Don't forget that shirts can be laundered in a day in most hotels. This is a lot easier than carrying an overloaded bag.

MICROPHONE SELECTION

Any time you speak to more than 30 people, you should use a microphone. It assures that everyone will hear and saves you from possible voice strain. A mike also promotes greater voice versatility. Even a whisper can be heard.

Each professional speaker has his or her own mike preference. Some use the hand held mike as a prop and have no problems with the cords involved.

I advise that if you speak a lot, you consider making an investment in your own wireless microphone.

A Wireless Microphone —

- Produces a higher quality sound.
- Allows for greater flexibility. A podium mike locks you into one location, partly hidden from your audience.
- Is packable. It fits into a briefcase or suitcase.
- Gives you freedom of mind.
- Is not a distraction. Some microphone systems can be a barrier between you and your audience. The wireless mike can be as small as the head of a pin. The transmitter which is about the size of a deck of cards can be in your pocket, clipped to your belt or under your jacket.
- Allows you to use a small cassette tape player to play music or tapes through the system.

One problem with wireless microphones is that you have to remember to turn them off. Recently, a pastor in one of the local churches was testing a new, wireless microphone system. He found out about the transmitting range when he forgot to turn it off as he went to the bathroom right before the second service.

YOUR VOICE

Your voice is your most important tool. Several days of presenting can put a strain on it. Here are some things you can do to prevent hoarseness.

- **Seat smokers near the back of the room.** Smoke is a major irritant of the throat. As the presenter, part of your room preparation can be to designate smoking spots. The non-smokers will also be grateful to choose where to sit.

- **Make sure you speak from the diaphragm.**

- **Hotel rooms are frequently very low in humidity, which causes dry throat.** When spending the night, run the shower for a bit, or put a wet towel over the blower unit to create more moisture in the air.

- **Don't eat dairy products before you speak.** Milk causes what is commonly called "cotton mouth."

- **Don't cough to get rid of "frogs."** This condition is usually caused by phlegm on the vocal cords. Coughing increases the irritation, thereby increasing the hoarseness. The correct method to handle this situation is to pant slightly and swallow.

- **Laryngitis is a concern** to people who speak a lot and reasonably so. It puts us out of business.

  > *Dr. Jack Smith, the family doctor, gave us the same advice he gave Hubert Humphrey when he asked for a quick cure for larangytis. "There's only one thing you can do — stop talking!" Hoarseness happens in your situation because the vocal cords swell. As soon as you can, give them a rest. Whisper if you must talk after your presentation. Whispering doesn't involve the vocal cords.*

For me, this sometimes means I have to forego a dinner engagement after the presentation. They expect you as the guest to talk, which could mean going from a hoarse voice to a total loss of voice. I have found that a gargle of 1/4 teaspoon salt to a glass of warm water is soothing. A drink of honey, tea, and lemon also eases the soreness that is the warning sign before laryngitis.

YOUR BODY

Monitor your health habits to maintain an abundance of energy. Presenting gives you a high, but it is energy-draining. Remember to use the basics of stretching to get your circulation going before you go on.

Check the hotels you stay in for exercise rooms or athletic clubs. An alternative to this is to carry your own cassette tape for aerobics in your room. Another even simpler solution for getting exercise is to climb the steps to your room. Few people do this so it gives you the freedom to run or take two at a time. Exercise will build up your body capacity for energy as well as relax you after a big presentation.

Many books have been written on nutrition and its effect on the body. It's an important topic! I suggest you read one or two so you can wisely choose the foods you want to eat to maintain maximum energy levels. Remember, too, that you can order special meals on the plane at no extra cost. The vegetable meal or fruit plate is a good light alternative.

YOUR PRESENTATION

If you speak a lot, chances are you are fairly comfortable up in front. This gives you the freedom to be a bit flexible with your material.

- If there are speakers before you, work some of what you've heard into your opening. This lets everyone know you were really present and not mentally in another place rehearsing.

- Prepare three different ways to make a point. When you feel the chemistry develop between you and your audience, you can decide which way is best for them.

- Risk each time you present! Present an old idea in a new way. This will keep you and your material alive and growing.

- Continue to tape yourself so you can critique your efforts. As a speaker you have a lot of leverage in the room. This gives you the corresponding reponsibility to be good!

Most importantly: No matter how good you get at presenting, you can never forget that you are there to *contribute, not to perform!*

SUMMARY

If you speak a lot, remember:

1. **Do** use visualization rehearsal method.

2. **Do** exercise to keep energy level high.

3. **Do** practice good nutrition to maintain stamina and physical presence.

4. **Do** contribute — don't perform.

5. **Do** receive critiques — evaluations.

6. **Do** tape yourself to find what to use again and what to dump.

7. **Do** risk new material — keep fresh.

8. **Do** be flexible with your material.

9. **Do** keep a file of your personal experiences by category.

10. **Do** realize the responsibility and leverage you have.

*   *   *   *   *   *   *

1. **Don't** get sloppy — neglecting mental preparation.

2. **Don't** stop personalizing your material to the audience.

3. **Don't** assume you know your audience.

4. **Don't** perform for your satisfaction — instead of the listener's benefit.

5. **Don't** assume that all details of equipment and material are correct. Check personally.

6. **Don't** get into a pattern of poor nutrition and exercise.

7. **Don't** get too slick — you lose touch with the listeners.

8. **Don't** assume that the scheduled location can't be changed if it isn't suitable.

9. **Don't** let frustration of travel take away from the thrill of speaking.

10. **Don't** forget Murphy — and O'Toole. If something can go wrong, it will!

CHAPTER 13

CONTRIBUTE — DON'T PERFORM!

This book was written with the Point of View that you will be a better presenter if you have focused content, correct content and are committed to your content. The benefits and facts have been detailed. It is time for you to ask "Now what?" It is time to talk about what you need to do!

There's the story about a man named Christopher Columbus. He had a dream: He wanted to sail around the world. He went to the usual channels for financial support. They laughed him off with "The world is flat." After the queen finally consented to be his backer, he went to get his ships. When they heard his plans, they added, "You're crazy" to "The world is flat." Getting a crew met with more verbal abuse. Everyone knew "The world is flat." Despite the jeering, Columbus persisted and with his single discovery proved they were all wrong.

What "flat worlds" are keeping you from being the best presenter you can be?

You will be the same person five years from now with the exception of:

The books you read

The people you meet

The places you go

The risks you take

Don't be content to be the same. Decide to grow with some of the ideas you got in this book. They concern skills you use every day of your life because any business person makes at least one presentation every day he or she works.

My job as a consultant is to get people to think. The more difficult challenge is to get them to **rethink**. You are already presenting. I've given you some ideas that will make you better. But you'll need to rethink, and to do things a little differently.

It's time for **reconceptualization.** Remember Father Weber, "To know and not do is to not know."

An Exercise

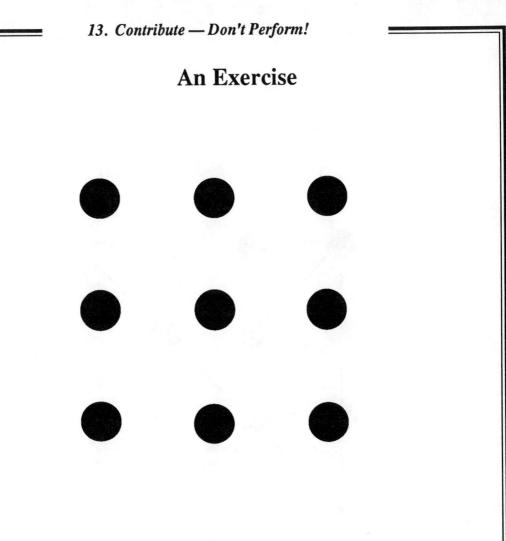

Directions: Connect all these dots with four straight connected lines, never taking your pencil off the paper.

(Solution on the next page)

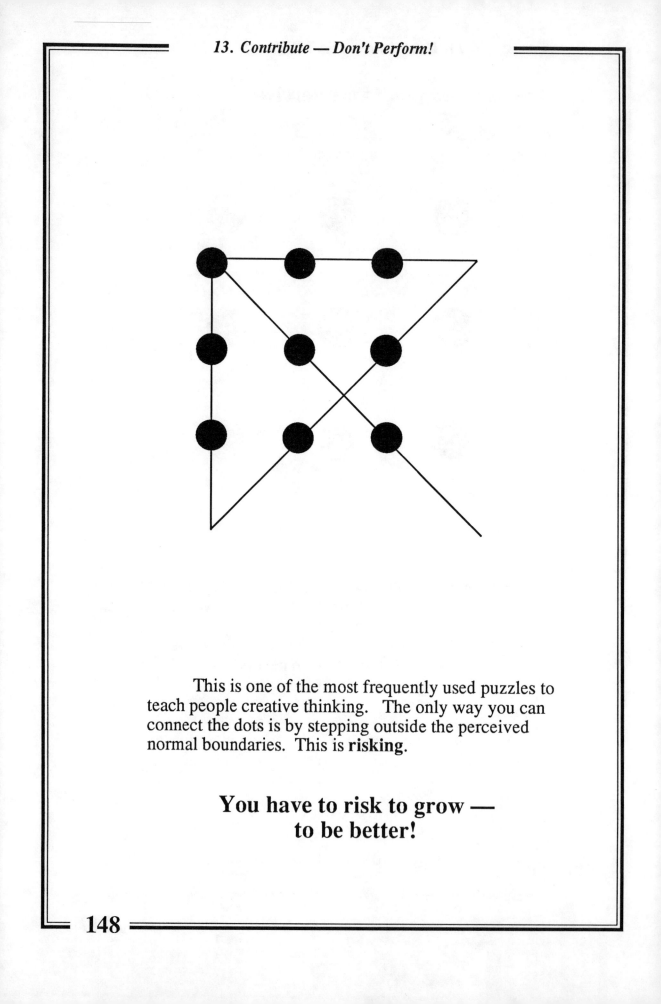

This is one of the most frequently used puzzles to teach people creative thinking. The only way you can connect the dots is by stepping outside the perceived normal boundaries. This is **risking**.

**You have to risk to grow —
to be better!**

One of the easiest ways to do this is to remember that in each presentation you are there **to contribute, not to perform**. You have something to give your audience whether that audience consists of one person or forty.

A number of years ago, my wife Judy and I had the opportunity to hear Father John Powell speak. He told the story of his first presentation to his fellow Jesuits. He had published many books and was a sought-after speaker. Yet, he had never been asked to address his own community.

The invitation finally came and he began to prepare. His goal was to "wow" them — to knock their socks off. He was incredibly nervous, which had never happened before. In desperation, he found a quiet place to pray about it. That was when it came to him: He'd been preparing to perform, not to contribute. When his focus changed, preparation was easy, and the talk was a success.

Three words define selling:

Selling is helping!

Any time you give a presentation where you expect something to happen, you are selling . You sell most effectively by helping, by contributing.

This desire to contribute is a natural result of a commitment to your audience. Pretense and polish are far less important than truly caring about your audience.

> **People don't care
> how much you know
> until they know how much you care.**

My father was in a nursing home for four years before he died. He had Alzheimer's Disease — a progressive degeneration of the brain. It took a while to figure out what to do when I visited him. He wouldn't greet me. Usually he said nothing — just sat with his head hanging. It was hard to know if he was comprehending anything I said. On one visit, I pulled out my calendar and started talking about my upcoming schedule. His head remained hanging as I went over plans, hopes and dreams. Then the moment happened that has remained my directive. He lifted his head and said the only words he'd said in weeks: "Then get on with it, son!"

It's time for you to "get on with it" if you are going to get better.

PROBLEM INDEX

If you are ...

PARTIAL LIST OF POSSIBLE BGO's
(in case you missed some)

1. Presentations are more than giving information.

2. You're more effective if you can communicate.

3. Good communication is a learnable skill.

4. Getting better means risking.

5. The first step in preparing is defining the audience.

6. The setting is part of the speaker's responsibility.

7. You can't organize content without first establishing a Point of View.

8. Point of View is the most important part of the content.

9. People buy benefits; a presentation needs benefits.

10. Don't drown the audience in too many facts.

11. Personal experiences are the most powerful content.

12. The recommendation has to tie into the Point of View.

13. Mental visualization of a POV outline will keep me on track.

14. It's possible to be an extemporaneous speaker.

15. Immersion presenting is the way to go!

16. AV materials can add substantially to retention of the presentation.

17. Use the keystone eliminator.

18. Use mega-pens for visuals!

19. Commitment to content will produce the energy needed to deliver content.

20. How you look adds to your believability!

21. Neutral position makes gestures easy.

22. Tension shows in your voice, but it's easy to fix.

23. Silence is better than non-words.

24. Eyes are the most important visual.

25. Commitment to content will overcome nervousness.

26. If you don't rehearse, you shouldn't present.

27. Personal stories are the best source of humor.

28. Try the exchange agenda!

29. Body language is important during question-and-answer time.

30. Every presentation should be a contribution, not a performance.

BIBLIOGRAPHY

Borden, Richard C.
<u>Public Speaking as Listeners Like It</u>.
Harper & Brothers, 1935.

Brembeck, Winston, and William Howell.
<u>Persuasion</u>.
Prentice-Hall, Inc., 1952.

Bryant, Donald Cross.
<u>Fundamentals of Public Speaking</u>.
Appleton, 1969.

Carnegie, Dale.
<u>The Quick and Easy Way to Effective Speaking</u>.
Pocket Books, 1962.

Crain, Sharon.
<u>Speaking Skills for the Professional</u> (audio cassette).
Educational Seminars Institute, 1983.

Decker, Bert.
<u>Speak To Win</u> (audio cassette program).
Decker Communications, Inc., 1985.

Dellinger, Susan.
<u>Communicating Effectively:</u>
<u>A Complete Guide for Better Managing</u>.
Chilton, 1980.

Ebninger, Douglas.
<u>Principles of Speech Communication</u>.
Scott, Foresman, 1980.

Fellows, Hugh Price.
<u>Business Speaking and Writing</u>.
Prentice-Hall, 1982.

Fettig, Art.
<u>How to Hold an Audience in the Hollow of Your Hand</u>.
Fell, 1979.

Fletcher, Leon.
<u>How to Design & Deliver a Speech</u>.
Harper & Row, 1979.

Fletcher, Leon.
    How to Speak Like a Pro.
    Ballantine Books, 1983.

Hanna, Michael S.
    Communicating in Business and Professional Settings.
    Random House, 1984.

Himstreet, William C.
    Business Communications: A Guide to Effective Writing,
    Speaking and Listening.
    Pitman Business Education, 1982.

Hoff, Ron.
    Presentation Techniques.
    Foote, Cone and Belding Communications, Inc., 1981.

Humes, James C.
    Instant Eloquence.
    Harper, 1973.

Kenny, Michael.
    Presenting Yourself.
    J. Wiley & Sons, 1982.

Leech, Thomas.
    How to Prepare, Stage and Deliver Winning Presentations.
    Amacom, 1982.

Lewis, David V.
    Secrets of Successful Writing, Speaking and Listening.
    Amacom, 1982.

Linkletter, Art.
    Public Speaking for Private People.
    Bobbs-Merrill, 1980.

Linver, Sandy.
    Speak and Get Results.
    Summit Books, 1983.

Linver, Sandy.
    Speak Easy.
    Summit Books, 1978.

Martel, Myles.
    Before You Say a Word: The Executive Guide to
    Effective Communication.
    Prentice-Hall, Inc., 1984.

Nickels, Harry G.
    <u>Do's and Don'ts for Writers and Speakers</u>.
    Greenwich House, 1983.

Powers, David Guy.
    <u>First Book of How to Make a Speech</u>.
    Watts, 1963.

Quebein, Nido R.
    <u>Communicate Like a Pro</u>.
    Berkley Books, 1983.

Quick, John.
    <u>I Hate to Make Speeches: Help for People Who Must</u>.
    Grosset, 1973.

Quick, John.
    <u>A Short Book on the Subject of Speaking</u>.
    Grosset, 1978.

Rogers, Natalie H.
    <u>Talk-Power: How to Speak Without Fear:</u>
    <u>A Systematic Training Program</u>.
    Dodd, Mead, 1982.

Sager, Arthur W.
    <u>Speak Your Way to Success</u>.
    McGraw-Hall, 1968.

Sarnoff, Dorothy.
    <u>Make the Most of Your Best</u>.
    Doubleday, 1981.

Sarnoff, Dorothy.
    <u>Speech Can Change Your Life</u>.
    Doubleday, 1970.

Shea, Gordon.
    <u>Managing a Difficult or Hostile Audience</u>.
    Prentice-Hall, 1984.

Valenti, Jack.
    <u>Speak Up With Confidence</u>.
    W. Morrow, 1982.

Van Oosting, James.
    <u>The Business Speech: Speaker, Audience, and Text</u>.
    Prentice-Hall, Inc., 1985.

Vasile, Albert J.
    <u>Speak With Confidence: A Practical Guide</u>.
    Winthrop Publishers, 1980.

Verderber, Rudolph F.
    The Challenge of Effective Speaking.
    Wadsworth Pub., 1970.

Von Oech, Roger.
    A Kick In The Seat Of The Pants.
    Warner, 1985.

Von Oech, Roger.
    A Whack On The Side Of The Head.
    Warner, 1985.

Waitley, Denis.
    The Winner's Edge.
    Berkley Books, 1980.

Weldon, Joel.
    Elephant's Don't Bite. (Audio Cassette).
    National Speaker's Association, 1981.

Westland, Peter.
    Public Speaking For Self-Improvement and Success.
    Arc, 1963.

Wohlmuth, Ed.
    The Overnight Guide To Public Speaking.
    Running Press, 1983.

ORDER BLANK

_____ **POV outlines** — 8-1/2 x 11 size — tablet form
25 sheets to a tablet.

$2.50 per tablet

_____ **Six Cassette Tape Programs With Workbook**

[ ] Presentation Skills for Accounting/Financial Professionals
[ ] Presentation Skills for Science/Engineering Professionals
[ ] Presentation Skills for Sales/Marketing Professionals
[ ] Presentation Skills for Senior Management
[ ] Presentation Skills for Advertising Professionals
[ ] Presentation Skills for Business Professionals

$69.95 U.S.A.
plus shipping   **4.50**

_____ **What's Your Point?**   **$12.95 U.S.A.**
$14.95 Canada
plus shipping   **2.00**

Please send information on:

_____ Presentation Skills Seminar/Workshop

_____ Coming to my company

_____ Other Services of Successful Presentations

NAME: _____

COMPANY: _____

ADDRESS: _____

CITY: _____STATE: _____ ZIP:_____

TELEPHONE: _____

FAX: _____

Send to: **Boylan Enterprises, Inc.**
3195 Casco Circle
Wayzata MN 55391
(612) 471-8917
Fax: (612) 471-8928

"The point of view outline

by itself is so easy to use and will have such a dramatic effect on your presentations right away. The rest of the book is a bonus!"

Robert Purcell — President
National Advertising Agency Network

"A valuable tool

for everyone who needs to rely on effective communication skills."

Paul Taylor — Vice President Information Services
International Multifoods

"Anyone who reads and heeds ...

Bob Boylan's ideas can improve his/her effectiveness by 25 to 50%!"

Donald B. Kraft — President
Evans/Kraft, Inc. Advertising & Public Relations

"Presentation ideas helped

our sales department go 100% over our annual projected increase".

Jamie Carr — Vice President
Wild Dunes Resort

"What's Your Point?" is innovation

in communication at its best. I have taken Bob's course ... and used his methods at all management levels. Bob's methods truly work and get results. Plus his method is exciting, it is direct and it is fun. I recommend this book highly."

Robert P. Mountain, Jr.
European Managing Director
Time Magazine

" The best analogy I can use

is that Bob took my one-hour newscast and condensed it to a more effective 30-second newsbrief before the listener changes channels on me! I now deliver a more exciting message with greater impact on my listeners."

Mike Wethington
National Manager Retail Systems
Dataserv